Better Homes & Gardens.

CHRISTMAS
FROM THE HEART.

Volume 26

Meredith Consumer Marketing
Des Moines, Iowa

CHRISTMAS
FROM THE HEART.

MEREDITH CORPORATION CONSUMER MARKETING
Consumer Marketing Product Director: Heather Sorensen
Consumer Marketing Product Manager: Tami Perkins
Consumer Products Marketing Manager: Wendy Merical
Business Manager: Diane Umland
Senior Production Manager: Al Rodruck

WATERBURY PUBLICATIONS, INC.
Contributing Editor: Carol Field Dahlstrom
Contributing Copy Editor: Carrie Truesdell
Contributing Proofreader: Terri Fredrickson
Contributing Photographer: Jacob Fox

Editorial Director: Lisa Kingsley
Creative Director: Ken Carlson
Associate Editor: Tricia Bergman
Associate Design Director: Doug Samuelson
Production Assistant: Mindy Samuelson

BETTER HOMES AND GARDENS· MAGAZINE
Editor in Chief: Stephen Orr
Creative Director: Jennifer D. Madara
Senior Deputy Editor: Nancy Wall Hopkins

MEREDITH PUBLISHING GROUP
President: Tom Harty

MEREDITH CORPORATION
Chairman and Chief Executive Officer: Stephen M. Lacy

In Memoriam: E.T. Meredith III (1933–2003)

All of us at Meredith Consumer Marketing are dedicated to
providing you with information and ideas to enhance your home.
We welcome your comments and suggestions. Write to us at:
Meredith Consumer Marketing, 1716 Locust St., Des Moines, IA 50309-3023.

Contents

OH, WHAT FUN!

Chances are you are humming a Christmas carol and planning your holiday party right now. Or maybe you are wrapping a handmade gift while you enjoy a cup of hot chocolate. We know you are as excited about Christmas as we are and we can help you get in the spirit with fresh ideas for decorating your holiday home, clever crafts you'll love to make and give, and delicious recipes that are sure to become your holiday favorites.

Love to entertain at holiday time? We have some super-special party nibbles and sips to share. Serve Panko Roasted Asparagus for a special treat or some Sweet Onion-Tomato Tartlets with a glass of Blackberry Fizz. Having house guests for the holidays? Make it easy by serving one-pan recipes and slow-cooker favorites such as Cheeseburger Shepherd's Pie and Chicken Soup with Chive Dumplings.

Is crafting your favorite part of the holidays? Gather your crafting supplies and enjoy making some special Plaid-Trimmed Mini Mittens to hang on your tree or to tie on a package. Or try your hand at making a Charming Gingerbread House using our templates and pretty papers. You can stitch up Softly Scented Sachets in less than an hour to give as special gifts that will be treasured. Or try creating an easy and elegant centerpiece using red pomegranates, fresh herbs, and scented candles.

Oh, what fun it is to celebrate this very best time of year with handmade projects and homemade treats to share with everyone you love. Make this the best Christmas ever, a *Christmas from the Heart*.

Perfectly Plaid

Tartan, gingham, or checked—whatever you prefer, you'll find the perfect plaid project to make just in time for Christmas.

ROUNDED-OUT TRIMS

Plaid strips of fabric are wound around a simple foam ball for a quick and easy holiday ornament.

WHAT YOU NEED

3-inch diameter foam ball such as Styrofoam • Scissors • Plaid fabrics in desired patterns and colors • Short straight pins • Paintbrush • Crafts glue • Red-and-white bakers twine

WHAT YOU DO

1. Plan the design of the ball by choosing the desired fabrics. Cut the fabric into ¾-inch-wide strips about 1 foot long. You will need about 4 feet of cut strips for each ball.

2. Use a straight pin to secure the fabric at one side. Brush a little glue onto the ball. Wrap the ball around and around, pressing down on the ball and allowing the glue to help tighten the fabric to the ball.

3. Make a loop using the bakers twine. Use a straight pin to secure to the top of the ornament. Let ornament dry.

PLAID-ALL-AROUND WREATH

Little pieces of plaid fabric combine with jingle bells and acorn tops to make an oh-so-plaid wreath for your front door.

WHAT YOU NEED

12-inch round foam wreath such as Styrofoam • Scissors • Plaid fabrics in desired patterns and colors • Awl or sharpened pencil • Crafts glue • Acorn tops • Jingle bells in desired colors • Bits of fresh greenery • 3-inch-wide ribbon for bow • Straight pins

WHAT YOU DO

1. Plan the design of the wreath by choosing the desired fabrics. Cut the fabric into 3½×3½-inch squares. You will need about 80 squares for a 12-inch wreath.

2. Fold the fabric squares in half and use the awl to poke the fabric into the foam, using a drop of glue to secure if needed. Continue until entire wreath is covered.

3. Glue the jingle bells into the acorn tops and let dry. Glue the acorn shapes onto the fabric where desired.

4. Tuck bits of greenery into the wreath.

5. Tie a large bow and pin to the wreath with straight pins.

Red and green plaid ribbons in all lengths and widths stack up with tiny pom-pom trim to form a simple Christmas tree shape. Double-stick tape keeps the ribbons in place and makes creating the card a quick and easy holiday project.

PLAID-WRAPPED LIGHT

A humble Mason jar lights up when a snippet of plaid ribbon is wrapped around it.

WHAT YOU NEED

Pint Mason jar • 1-inch-wide plaid ribbon • Double-stick tape • Scissors • Twine • Small piece of greenery • Votive candle

WHAT YOU DO

1. Be sure the jar is clean and dry.
2. Wrap the ribbon around the jar and secure with double-stick tape. Trim ends.
3. Tie a piece of twine around the jar and secure with a bow. Add a piece of fresh greenery.
4. Place the candle inside the jar.

Never leave a burning candle unattended.

RIBBON-TREE GREETING

Scraps of plaid ribbon are lined up to make a clever card to share for the holidays.

WHAT YOU NEED

Blank card and envelope in kraft brown • Narrow plaid ribbons in desired colors and designs • Scissors • Double-stick tape • Small scraps of small pom-pom trim • Small adhesive-back star

WHAT YOU DO

1. Plan the design of the card. Cut small pieces of ribbon and lay them on the card to form a tree shape.
2. Use double-stick tape to secure each piece of ribbon and pom-pom trim on the card front.
3. Add a star at the top of the tree.
4. Trim the envelope with a piece of ribbon if desired.

PIN-TUCKED PLAID STOCKING

With tiny tucks, a plain-color cuff combines with a bold plaid to make an heirloom-quality stocking.

WHAT YOU NEED

Tracing paper • Pencil • ½ yard plaid or checked taffeta fabric for stocking body • ½ yard black lining fabric for stocking lining and backing for tucked pieces • ¼ yard black taffeta fabric for cuff, heel, and toe • Scissors • Thread to match fabrics

WHAT YOU DO

1. Enlarge and trace pattern, right, and cut out. Draw separate pieces for the toe and heel, adding a ⅜-inch seam to the pattern pieces. Cut out. Cut two stocking patterns from plaid fabric, reversing one. Repeat for the stocking lining. Cut one piece from lining fabric for the heel and toe. In addition, cut two 8×4-inch pieces from taffeta fabric to pin tuck for the heel and toe. Set aside.

2. For the cuff, cut two 4×7-inch pieces of black lining fabric and one 4×7-inch piece of black taffeta fabric for the back cuff. Cut another 4×14-inch piece of taffeta fabric to pin tuck for the cuff front.

3. Pin-tuck the cuff, toe, and heel taffeta pieces by using the lining pieces as guides. Pin-tuck the black taffeta fabric by ironing tucks into the fabric and sewing in place using a straight stitch. Trim the tucked pieces to match the lining pieces and baste together, treating the pieces as one piece. Baste the back cuff lining and back cuff taffeta together and treat as one piece.

4. Turn under the edges of the toe and heel, and sew to the stocking front using a straight stitch.

5. Stitch front and back stocking pieces with right sides together, leaving top edges open using ½-inch seam. Clip curves. Turn right side out. Press.

6. Stitch lining pieces with right sides together using a ½-inch seam. Turn right side out. Insert lining inside turned stocking, keeping top straight edges even and wrong sides together. Baste across top of stocking with lining in place.

7. Pin cuff pieces right sides together and stitch on short sides; turn. Machine hem one side of cuff. With right sides together, slide cuff over top of stocking, raw edges even, and pin in place. Stitch. Remove pins; bring cuff up and press. Turn back top of cuff and press. Add hanging loop if desired.

Pin-Tucked Plaid Stocking Pattern

Enlarge 200%

PLAID-TRIMMED MINI MITTENS

Scraps of white wool are trimmed with taffeta plaid prints, simple stitches, and gold buttons to make a mini-mitten garland and holiday trims.

WHAT YOU NEED

Tracing paper • Pencil • Scissors • White wool • Small pieces of taffeta plaid print fabric • Red embroidery thread • Needle • Small gold button • Cording

WHAT YOU DO

1. Trace the patterns, right and below, add a ⅜-inch seam allowance to all pieces and cut out. Cut two mitten body pieces from white wool. Cut one cuff piece from plaid taffeta.
2. With mitten pieces right sides together, starting at the top, stitch three-fourths way down the long side of the mitten; open up. With right sides together, stitch the cuff to the top of the mitten. Press flat.
3. Embroider little "X"s on the front of the mitten. Fold mitten and cuff right sides together and stitch around mitten. Turn and press. Fold cuff under and stitch in place.
4. Sew a gold button at the corner of the mitten. Add a loop for an ornament or a cord for a garland.

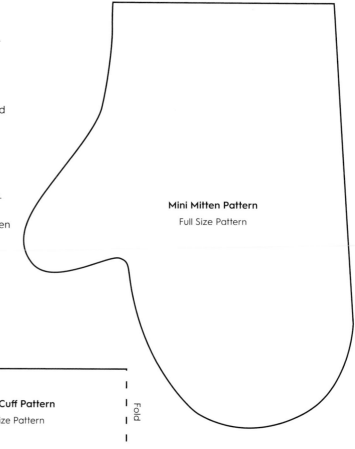

Mini Mitten Pattern

Full Size Pattern

Mitten Cuff Pattern

Full Size Pattern

Fold

PATCHWORK PLAID PILLOWS
Little squares of plaid flannel are sewn together patchwork style to make cozy Christmas pillows.

WHAT YOU NEED
Flannel in desired patterns and colors • Scissors • 12½-inch square batting • 12½-inch square muslin • 1½ yards piping-style cording • 12½-inch square fabric for backing • 12-inch pillow form or polyester fiberfill to stuff pillow cover

WHAT YOU DO
1. Plan the desired patchwork pattern or refer to the photo for ideas. Cut squares and triangles of flannel in desired colors. Sew shapes together to complete a 12½-inch pillow top using the pieces.

2. Layer top, batting, and muslin pieces together. Quilt as desired. Press.
3. For piping, cut fabric into 2-inch bias strips to cover cording. Join together to make an approximately 54-inch-long strip. Wrap fabric around cording, wrong sides together. Sew closely to cording using a zipper foot. Sew cording to pillow top, keeping raw edges of cording even with raw edges of top.
4. With right sides together, stitch the pillow top to the backing fabric, leaving a 6-inch opening to insert the pillow form or to stuff. Trim corners; turn right side out.
5. Insert pillow form or stuff pillow as desired. Stitch opening closed using matching thread and invisible hand stitches.

PLAID-DECKED CANDLES

A cherished enamel kitchen container becomes the center of attention when it is filled with candles and greens. Layer plaid ribbon over a fringed piece of burlap and tie around the container. Tie a bow with the ribbon. Set the candles in place and surround the candles with fresh evergreen clippings and holly.

WRAPPED-IN-PLAID TABLESCAPE

Create a tabletop with plaid in mind. Start with a plaid place mat and napkin, and then stack square and round white and striped dishes. Tie a plaid ribbon around the dishes. Add a little package name tag at each place setting using scraps of plaid ribbon and adhesive letters. Tuck a piece of greenery under the package.

MAD-ABOUT-PLAID PACKAGE TRIMS

Plaid becomes the theme for special packages tied up in ribbons with clever add-on toppers.

CASCADING STARS

Purchased paper stars on a string make the perfect addition to a neutral plaid-wrapped package. Christmas-red plaid ribbon wraps around the box, all tied in a traditional bow.

VINTAGE LIGHTS

On-the-bias plaid paper sets the stage for a simple retro wrap. Red and green vintage Christmas lights and a simple tag are tied on with bakers twine for a fun package addition.

STACKED UP

Why settle for just one package when two will do? For a quick wrap layer two packages together and tie up with plaid ribbon, a button-topped tag, and some fresh greenery.

CURLY TOPPED

Snippets of plaid ribbon are point-cut and tucked into the package lid for a quick holiday touch. The package is then topped with purchased curled ribbon, a quick tag, and a sticker to complete the all-plaid wrap.

COOKIE-CUTTER WRAP

Black-and-white and winter green are the theme of this plaid wrap. Two packages are stacked and then tied with black-and-white ribbon. An all-white snowman cookie cutter becomes a topper tie-on.

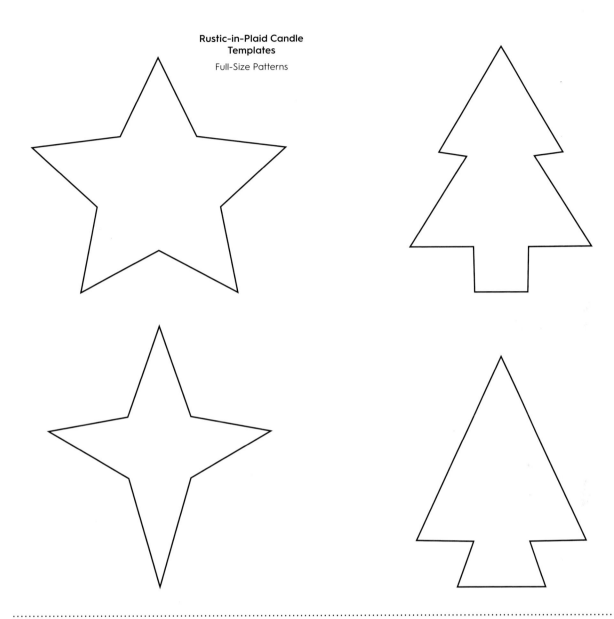

Rustic-in-Plaid Candle Templates

Full-Size Patterns

RUSTIC-IN-PLAID CANDLE

Bark from a tree is wrapped around a glass container to make a rustic candle for your table or mantel.

WHAT YOU NEED
• Tracing paper • Pencil• Glass candleholder • Water and small pail • Tree bark • Crafts knife • Scissors or tin snips • Hot-glue gun and glue sticks • Strong rubber bands • Plaid ribbon • Candle

WHAT YOU DO
1. Trace the desired pattern, above. Set aside.
2. Soak the bark in water until pliable.
3. Measure the height and circumference of the glass container. Add 2 inches to the circumference.

4. Use these measurements to cut the bark with a crafts knife, scissors, or tin snips. Lay the pattern on the bark on a cutting surface. Use the crafts knife to cut out the shape.
5. Wrap the bark around the glass container and hot-glue to secure. Place rubber bands around the container to hold the bark in place until dry. Remove rubber bands when dry.
6. Wrap the ribbon around the top and bottom of the container and secure in place with hot glue. Place candle in the container.

Never leave a burning candle unattended.

Let's Party— Bite by Bite!

Whether it's the entire neighborhood or an intimate few, planned or spontaneous, a holiday buffet or a nibble to enjoy over a leisurely visit, these festive appetizers and drinks will fill the bill for whatever type of gathering you're in the mood for—or for whoever walks through your door!

ASIAGO CHEESE DIP

Dried mushrooms will add more intense mushroom flavor to this Italian-style dip. Serve with Pinot Noir or apple cider for a perfect party pairing.

WHAT YOU NEED

- 1   cup chicken broth or water
- 4   oz. dried tomatoes (not oil-packed)
- 2   16-oz. cartons sour cream
- 1½   cups finely shredded Asiago cheese (6 oz.)
- 1¼   cups mayonnaise
- ½   8-oz. pkg. cream cheese, cut up
- 1   cup sliced fresh mushrooms or 1 oz. rehydrated dried mushrooms (such as porcini, shiitake, chanterelle, and/or oyster)*
- 1   cup thinly sliced green onions
      Baguette-style French bread slices, topped with finely shredded Asiago cheese and toasted

WHAT YOU DO

1. In a small saucepan bring broth to boiling. Remove from heat. Add dried tomatoes; cover and let stand 5 minutes. Drain, discarding liquid. Chop tomatoes (you should have about 1¼ cups).

2. Meanwhile, in a 3½- or 4-qt. slow cooker combine the next six ingredients (through green onions). Stir in chopped tomatoes.

3. Cover and cook on low 3 to 4 hours or on high 1½ to 2 hours. Stir well before serving. If desired, keep warm in the slow cooker on low up to 2 hours. If desired, sprinkle dip with additional thinly sliced green onions. Serve with toasted cheese-topped baguette slices. Makes 28 servings.

*Test Kitchen Tip To rehydrate dried mushrooms, place the dried mushrooms in a small bowl. Add enough boiling water to cover; let stand 30 minutes. Drain mushrooms, squeezing out any excess liquid. Coarsely chop mushrooms.

PANKO ROASTED ASPARAGUS

For crispy, tender asparagus, choose asparagus with firm, bright green stalks. If the stems are tough, use a vegetable peeler to remove the outer layer.

WHAT YOU NEED

1	lb. thick asparagus spears
½	cup mayonnaise
¼	cup Dijon-style mustard
2	tsp. lemon juice
1	cup panko bread crumbs
2	Tbsp. peanut oil

WHAT YOU DO

1. Preheat oven to 425°F. Snap off and discard woody bases from asparagus. If desired, scrape off scales. In a small bowl combine mayonnaise, mustard, and lemon juice. Transfer half of the mixture to a small serving bowl; cover and chill until ready to serve.

2. Place bread crumbs in a shallow dish. Spread the remaining mayonnaise mixture over asparagus spears; roll in bread crumbs to coat. Place in an ungreased 15×10×1-inch baking pan. Drizzle with oil.

3. Roast about 12 minutes or until asparagus is crisp-tender and bread crumbs are golden brown. Serve asparagus with the reserved mayonnaise mixture. Makes 16 servings.

CRAB AND HORSERADISH HAVARTI DIP

Guests coming over? No need to fret about last-minute prep. Make this dip ahead, then cover, refrigerate, and bake just before serving.

WHAT YOU NEED

1	8-oz. pkg. cream cheese, softened
1¼	cups shredded horseradish and chive Havarti cheese (5 oz.)*
⅓	cup sour cream
¼	cup mayonnaise
1	cup cooked lump crabmeat, flaked, or one 6-oz. can crabmeat, drained, flaked, and cartilage removed
1	cup shredded fresh baby spinach
	Breadsticks and/or other assorted breads

WHAT YOU DO

1. Preheat oven to 350°F. In a large bowl beat cream cheese, Havarti cheese, sour cream, and mayonnaise with a mixer on medium until combined. Gently stir in crabmeat and spinach.

2. Spread dip in an ungreased 1-qt. souffle dish or baking dish. Bake 25 minutes or until heated through. Serve dip with breadsticks and/or other assorted breads. Makes 12 servings.

*Test Kitchen Tip If you can't find the horseradish and chive Havarti cheese, substitute 1¼ cups shredded Havarti cheese and add 1 Tbsp. snipped fresh chives and 2 tsp. prepared horseradish with the sour cream.

PETITE PESTO-PARMESAN POTATOES

One potato, two potato...these tiny stuffed potatoes are sure to be a hit at your next party! Use either red or white new potatoes, or a combination of both for a colorful platter.

WHAT YOU NEED

- 20   tiny new potatoes (about 2¼ lb.)
- 4   oz. pancetta, chopped
- ⅔   cup light sour cream
- 2   tsp. snipped fresh chives
- ¼   tsp. salt
- ¼   tsp. cracked black pepper
- ¼   cup refrigerated basil pesto
- ¼   cup shredded Parmesan cheese (1 oz.)
       Snipped fresh chives (optional)
       Cracked black pepper (optional)

WHAT YOU DO

1. Preheat oven to 425°F. Prick potatoes with a fork. Arrange potatoes in a 15×10×1-inch baking pan. Bake 20 to 30 minutes or until tender, stirring once.

2. Meanwhile, in a small skillet cook pancetta over medium heat until crisp. Drain pancetta on paper towels.

3. When potatoes are cool enough to handle, cut potatoes in half lengthwise. If necessary, cut a thin slice from each bottom to keep potato upright. Using a measuring teaspoon, scoop pulp out of each potato half, leaving a ¼-inch-thick shell. Place pulp in a medium bowl.

4. Mash the potato pulp with a potato masher or a mixer on low. Add sour cream, the 2 tsp. chives, the salt, and the ¼ tsp. pepper; beat until smooth. Spoon pesto into potato shells. Top with the mashed potato mixture. Place potato shells in a 3-qt. rectangular baking dish. Sprinkle with pancetta.

5. Bake about 5 minutes or until heated through. Sprinkle with cheese. Bake about 2 minutes more or until cheese melts. If desired, top with additional chives and cracked pepper. Makes 40 servings.

SWEET ONION-TOMATO TARTLETS

Onions and grape tomatoes are roasted with rosemary for a sweet and savory filling.

WHAT YOU NEED

- 3   cups grape tomatoes
- 1   sweet onion, quartered and thinly sliced (about 2 cups)
- 2   Tbsp. olive oil
- 1   Tbsp. snipped fresh rosemary
- ½   tsp. salt
- ½   tsp. black pepper
- 1   Tbsp. sherry vinegar
- 1   17.3-oz. pkg. frozen puff pastry sheets, thawed (2 sheets)
       Manchego or Parmigiano-Reggiano cheese, shaved

WHAT YOU DO

1. Preheat oven to 400°F. Prick tomatoes with a fork or the tip of a sharp knife. In a 15×10×1-inch baking pan combine tomatoes and the next five ingredients (through pepper). Roast 25 to 30 minutes or until onion is tender. Remove from oven. Sprinkle with vinegar; let cool.

2. Meanwhile, line a large baking sheet with parchment paper. On a lightly floured surface, unfold puff pastry. Using a 3-inch round cookie cutter, cut nine rounds from each sheet (18 total). Place rounds on the prepared baking sheet.

3. Spoon about 2 Tbsp. of the roasted tomato mixture on each pastry round. Bake 15 to 20 minutes or until edges are puffed and golden brown. Let stand 5 minutes before serving. Top with shaved cheese. Makes 18 servings.

RICH NORWEGIAN MEATBALLS

Brewed coffee in both the meatballs and sauce gives these Nordic-style meatballs rich flavor.

WHAT YOU NEED

1½	cups soft bread crumbs
½	cup half-and-half
1¼	cups strong coffee
2	eggs, lightly beaten
½	cup finely chopped onion
¼	cup finely snipped fresh Italian parsley
1½	tsp. salt
2	tsp. freshly grated nutmeg
¼	tsp. black pepper
1	lb. lean ground beef
½	lb. uncooked ground turkey breast and/or lean ground pork
¼	cup butter
¼	cup all-purpose flour
1	cup beef broth

WHAT YOU DO

1. In a large bowl combine bread crumbs, half-and-half, and ¼ cup of the coffee. Let stand until mixture is evenly moist.

2. Add eggs, onion, parsley, 1 tsp. of the salt, 1 tsp. of the nutmeg, and the pepper. Add beef and turkey; mix well. Cover and chill 2 hours. With moistened hands, shape mixture into 72 meatballs.

3. In an extra-large skillet melt 2 Tbsp. of the butter over medium heat. Cook half of the meatballs in hot butter about 12 minutes or until done (165°F),* carefully turning to brown evenly. With a slotted spoon, remove meatballs from skillet. Add remaining butter to skillet and repeat with remaining meatballs. Remove meatballs from skillet.

4. Stir flour into pan drippings until smooth. Add broth, the remaining 1 cup coffee, 1 tsp. nutmeg, and ½ tsp. salt. Cook and stir over medium heat until thickened and bubbly.

5. Return all meatballs to skillet; heat through, gently stirring occasionally. Makes 72 servings.

Make-Ahead Directions Prepare as directed through Step 4. Layer meatballs in a freezer container between sheets of waxed paper. Transfer sauce to a freezer container. Label and freeze up to 3 months. Thaw sauce and meatballs in the refrigerator overnight. In an extra-large skillet bring sauce to a simmer over medium heat. Sauce will appear curdled at first but will become smooth as it heats up. Add meatballs. Cover and simmer about 8 minutes or until heated through.

*Test Kitchen Tip The internal color of a meatball is not a reliable doneness indicator. A beef-and-turkey meatball cooked to 165°F is safe, regardless of color. To measure the doneness of a meatball, insert an instant-read thermometer into the center of the meatball.

PEPPERCORN PASTRIES WITH BEEF

When you need a nibble with a little elegance, these mounds of peppery roast beef and a horseradish-flavor sour cream on pillows of puff pastry are the perfect pick.

WHAT YOU NEED

1	17.3-oz. pkg. frozen puff pastry sheets, thawed (2 sheets)
1	egg, lightly beaten
1	tsp. water
1	8-oz. carton sour cream
2	Tbsp. assorted snipped fresh herbs (such as basil, oregano, thyme, dill, and/or parsley)
4	tsp. prepared horseradish
1	clove garlic, minced
8	oz. very thinly sliced deli roast beef, torn into pieces
1	tsp. cracked peppercorn melange or cracked black pepper
	Assorted fresh herbs

WHAT YOU DO

1. Preheat oven to 375°F. Lightly grease two baking sheets or line with parchment paper. On a lightly floured surface, unfold puff pastry sheets. Roll each sheet into a 15×10-inch rectangle. Cut crosswise into nine 1½-inch-wide strips; cut strips crosswise into thirds (54 total). Place pastry rectangles about 1 inch apart on the prepared baking sheets.

2. Combine egg and the water. Lightly brush pastry rectangles with egg mixture. Bake 8 to 10 minutes or until lightly browned. Cool on wire racks.

3. For topping, stir together sour cream, the 2 Tbsp. snipped herbs, the horseradish, and garlic.

4. To serve, spread about 1 tsp. of the topping on each pastry rectangle. Mound beef on top of pastry. Sprinkle with peppercorn melange and top with additional fresh herbs. Makes 54 servings.

of phyllo; coat with cooking spray. Repeat with two more sheets of phyllo, coating each with cooking spray. Cut the phyllo stack in half lengthwise. Cut each half-stack crosswise into thirds (six rectangles total). Press each rectangle into a prepared muffin cup. Repeat to make six more phyllo cups, using the remaining phyllo and coating each sheet with cooking spray.

3. Coat the insides of the phyllo cups with cooking spray. Place a cheese round in each phyllo cup. Sprinkle with Italian seasoning and pepper.

4. Bake about 8 minutes or until phyllo is golden brown. Cool in pan on a wire rack 10 minutes. Remove phyllo cups from muffin pan. Spoon Bruschetta Topper into phyllo cups. Serve warm. Makes 12 servings.

Bruschetta Topper In a medium bowl combine ½ cup chopped pitted Kalamata olives; ¼ cup chopped tomato; 1 Tbsp. snipped fresh basil; 1 Tbsp. chopped bottled roasted red sweet pepper; 1 Tbsp. chopped green onion; 1 Tbsp. finely chopped carrot; 1 Tbsp. finely chopped celery; 1 Tbsp. olive oil; 1 tsp. snipped fresh parsley; 1 tsp. lemon zest; 1 tsp. balsamic vinegar; 2 cloves garlic, minced; ⅛ tsp. salt; ⅛ tsp. dried oregano, crushed; and ⅛ tsp. black pepper.

MARYLAND CRAB CAKES

You can use either fresh or canned crab to make this classic appetizer. If using canned crab, choose backfin crabmeat—it's less expensive than lump crabmeat, but still has the sweet flavor and enough texture for great-tasting cakes.

WHAT YOU NEED

1   egg, lightly beaten
2   Tbsp. mayonnaise
1   Tbsp. snipped fresh parsley
2   tsp. Old Bay Seasoning (seafood seasoning)
1½   tsp. snipped fresh thyme
2   slices soft white bread
1   lb. cooked lump crabmeat or three 6-oz. cans crabmeat, drained and cartilage removed
1   Tbsp. peanut oil or vegetable oil
     Bottled tartar sauce (optional)

WHAT YOU DO

1. In a large bowl combine the first five ingredients (through thyme). Remove and discard crusts from bread. Tear bread into very small pieces; stir into egg mixture. Add crabmeat; gently mix with your hands, keeping crab pieces whole. Shape crab mixture into twelve ½-inch-thick patties.

2. In a large nonstick skillet heat oil over medium heat. Add half of the crab cakes; cook about 6 minutes or until golden brown and heated through, turning once. If cakes brown too quickly reduce heat to medium-low. Keep warm in a 300°F oven while cooking the remaining crab cakes (add additional oil, if necessary).

3. If desired, serve crab cakes with tartar sauce. Makes 12 servings.

PHYLLO-CRUSTED CHEESE WITH BRUSCHETTA TOPPER

Tiny, preformed cheese rounds are the perfect size to fill these tartlets. Select a cheese that's mild in flavor to best pair with the balsamic-veggie topping.

WHAT YOU NEED

     Nonstick cooking spray
8   sheets frozen phyllo dough (14×9-inch rectangles), thawed
12   miniature wax-wrapped light semisoft cheese rounds, unwrapped
1   tsp. dried Italian seasoning, crushed
¼   tsp. black pepper
1   recipe Bruschetta Topper or ¾ cup refrigerated bruschetta topper plus 2 tsp. white or regular balsamic vinegar

WHAT YOU DO

1. Preheat oven to 400°F. Lightly coat twelve 2½-inch muffin cups with cooking spray.

2. Unfold phyllo dough; place one sheet of phyllo on a clean work surface. (As you work, keep the remaining phyllo dough covered with plastic wrap to prevent it from drying out.) Lightly coat phyllo with cooking spray. Top with another sheet

PARMESAN HAM AND CHEESE TOASTS

For the crowning touch to these cheesy toasts, top with a spoonful of peach or apricot preserves or a thin slice of apple or pear.

WHAT YOU NEED

2   Tbsp. butter
2   Tbsp. olive oil
1   clove garlic, minced
1   10-oz. loaf baguette-style French bread, cut diagonally into ¼-inch slices
18   Canadian-style bacon slices, cut in half
1½   cups shredded mozzarella cheese (6 oz.)
½   cup finely shredded Parmigiano-Reggiano cheese (2 oz.)
     Peach or apricot preserves (optional)

WHAT YOU DO

1. Preheat oven to 400°F. In a small saucepan combine butter, oil, and garlic. Cook over medium heat until butter melts. Remove from heat.

2. Brush butter mixture lightly over both sides of bread slices. Arrange bread slices in a single layer on a large baking sheet. Bake 6 to 8 minutes or until golden. Top each slice with a half-slice of Canadian bacon. Combine the mozzarella and Parmigiano-Reggiano cheese; sprinkle cheese over bacon slices.

3. Return slices to oven for 5 to 6 minutes more or until cheese is melted and bubbly. If desired, top with preserves while toasts are still warm. Makes 36 servings.

PROSCIUTTO-WRAPPED
HONEY-LEMON SHRIMP

This two-bite appetizer will be a favorite at any gathering. Serve the shrimp on a platter with a drizzle of honey or with slices of melon for a colorful garnish.

WHAT YOU NEED
24 fresh or frozen jumbo shrimp in shells (about 1 lb.)
1   lemon
2   Tbsp. honey
2   tsp. snipped fresh parsley
6   very thin slices prosciutto (4 to 5 oz.)

WHAT YOU DO
1. Thaw shrimp, if frozen. Preheat broiler. Peel and devein shrimp, leaving tails intact. Rinse shrimp; pat dry with paper towels. Place shrimp in a large bowl. Remove ½ tsp. zest and squeeze 2 Tbsp. juice from lemon. In a small bowl combine lemon zest and juice, the honey, and parsley. Pour over shrimp; toss gently to coat.
2. Cut prosciutto slices in half crosswise and then in half lengthwise (24 pieces total). Wrap a piece of prosciutto around each shrimp; secure with a wooden toothpick.
3. Place shrimp on the lightly greased unheated rack of a broiler pan. Broil 4 to 5 inches from the heat 4 to 6 minutes or until shrimp are opaque and prosciutto is crisp, turning once.
4. If desired, sprinkle shrimp with additional lemon zest and snipped fresh parsley, and serve with additional honey for dipping. Makes 8 servings.

BLACKBERRY FIZZ

Cheers to both sparkling wine and brandy in this fruity holiday sparkler!

WHAT YOU NEED
4   or 5 fresh blackberries or frozen unsweetened blackberries, thawed
½   oz. (1 Tbsp.) lime juice
1   tsp. superfine sugar
1½   oz. (3 Tbsp.) Cognac or other brandy
     Ice cubes
1½   oz. (3 Tbsp.) sparkling wine, chilled
     Blackberries
     Fresh mint sprig (optional)

WHAT YOU DO
1. In a cocktail shaker combine the 4 or 5 blackberries, the lime juice, and sugar. To muddle, gently crush berries with the back of a spoon. Add Cognac and ice cubes; cover and shake until the outside of the shaker becomes frosty. Strain into an ice-filled glass. Add sparkling wine. Top with additional blackberries and, if desired, a mint sprig. Makes 1 serving.

COGNAC-MARMALADE CHAMPAGNE COCKTAIL

A splash of Champagne and marmalade makes this brandy cocktail extra special.

WHAT YOU NEED

2   oz. (¼ cup) Cognac or other brandy
2   Tbsp. orange marmalade
2   oz. (¼ cup) Champagne, chilled
     Orange slice
     Fresh mint sprig

WHAT YOU DO

1. In a chilled cocktail glass combine Cognac and marmalade. Pour in Champagne. Add orange slice, a mint sprig, and a swizzle stick for stirring. Makes 1 serving.

CUBANA COGNAC

Fresh lemon and lime juices with a hint of mint create a refreshing base for this drink. Slightly crush the mint with the back of a spoon or muddler to release its flavor.

WHAT YOU NEED

1   Tbsp. sugar
½   oz. (1 Tbsp.) lemon juice
½   oz. (1 Tbsp.) lime juice
6   to 8 fresh mint leaves
2   oz. (¼ cup) Cognac or other brandy
     Ice
⅓   to ½ cup club soda, chilled (optional)
     Lemon and/or lime wedges (optional)

WHAT YOU DO

1. In a highball glass combine sugar, lemon juice, and lime juice, stirring to dissolve sugar. Add mint. To muddle, gently crush mint with the back of a spoon. Add Cognac. Fill the highball glass with ice. If desired, slowly pour in club soda; stir gently to combine. If desired, add lemon and/or lime wedges. **Shaker Directions** In a cocktail shaker combine sugar, lemon juice, and lime juice. Add mint. To muddle, gently crush mint with the back of a spoon. Add Cognac; fill three-fourths full with ice. Cover and shake until the outside of the shaker becomes frosty. Strain into a chilled cocktail glass (omit club soda). If desired, add lemon and/or lime wedges. Makes 1 serving.

COGNAC GRAPEFRUIT COCKTAIL

Although limoncello you make yourself tastes fresher and is less sweet than purchased limoncello, you can certainly swap the storebought stuff for homemade.

WHAT YOU NEED
    Lemon wedge
    Coarse decorating sugar
    Ice
2   oz. (¼ cup) grapefruit juice
1½ oz. (3 Tbsp.) Cognac or other brandy
½   oz. (1 Tbsp.) Limoncello (recipe, below)
½   oz. (1 Tbsp.) Cointreau or orange liqueur
½   oz. (1 Tbsp.) lemon juice
    Orange and/or lemon slices

WHAT YOU DO

1. Moisten the rim of a chilled cocktail glass with a lemon wedge and coat with sugar.

2. Fill a cocktail shaker three-fourths full with ice. Add grapefruit juice, Cognac, Limoncello, Cointreau, and lemon juice. Cover and shake until the outside of the shaker becomes frosty. Strain into the cocktail glass. If desired, add orange and/or lemon slices. Makes 1 serving.

Limoncello Scrub 10 lemons with a vegetable brush. Using a vegetable peeler, carefully cut enough yellow peel away from white pith to make 2 cups. (If desired, juice lemons and reserve for another use.) In a large glass pitcher or bowl combine 2 cups lemon peel and one 750-ml bottle vodka. Cover tightly and let stand in a cool, dry place 10 days, gently swirling mixture in pitcher each day. Strain mixture through a fine-mesh sieve; discard lemon peel. Return the lemon-infused vodka to pitcher. For syrup, in a medium saucepan combine 3 cups sugar and 2½ cups water. Bring just to boiling, stirring to dissolve sugar. Cool to room temperature. Pour syrup into lemon-infused vodka; stir to combine. Cover and chill overnight. Pour Limoncello through a funnel into clean bottles; secure lids. Store in the refrigerator up to 1 month. Makes about 7 cups.

Cognac is considered to be one of the finest types of brandy. True Cognac is made according to specific methods within the Cognac region of France. It begins with fermenting the juice of wine grapes, then distilling and aging in oak barrels to develop its wonderful complex flavors and gold-to-amber color.

Gingerbread
Inspired

Jolly gingerbread motifs are the inspiration for the projects in this catch-me-if-you-can chapter.

A humble cardboard box is cut into simple shapes and pieced together with bright paper straws and snippets of paper to create a sweet little gingerbread cottage that is just too cute to resist.

CHARMING GINGERBREAD HOUSE
A gingerbread house made from cardboard and happy paper trims will become the star at your holiday table.

WHAT YOU NEED
Pencil • Cardboard box • Crafts knife such as X-acto and cutting mat • Hot-glue gun and glue sticks • Cardstock in red, teal, and white, (one piece each) • Red-and-white stripe paper straws • Red-and-white stripe washi tape • Scissors

WHAT YOU DO
1. Trace patterns, opposite, and cut out. Cut pieces out of cardboard. Attach the cardboard pieces together with hot glue, working in sections referring to photo for placement.
2. To make peppermint candies, cut 1-inch circles out of red or teal and white paper. Cut white circle into sixths. Attach three of the sections onto the red circle using a hot-glue gun. When dry, attach peppermint to top of straw. Cut straws to desired length and attach to house front using hot glue.
3. To make roof candies, cut 1-inch circles out of white paper. Cut ¼×¼-inch squares from red paper and small circles from teal paper. Attach with hot glue. Embellish with washi tape as desired. Add a dot of red paper for the door handle.

Square Side
3×3 inches
cut 2

Charming Gingerbread
House Templates
Full-Size

Angled Side
cut 2

Roof
2¾×3½ inches
cut 2

Bottom
3×2⅞ inches

Door

Door Window

Windows
¾×¾ inches
cut 4 per side

APPLIQUÉ SKATING GINGERBREAD MEN

Gingerbread men are appliquéd to skate around an oval mat that can be used as a happy centerpiece for the holidays.

WHAT YOU NEED

Finished size: 15×21-inch oval

½ yard off-white cotton snowflake print for background and backing • 1 fat quarter burgundy cotton print for hats, boots, and binding • 12-inch square rich brown cotton print for gingerbread men • 6-inch square medium teal cotton print for scarves • ½ yard paper-backed fusible web • 22×16-inch stabilizer • Twelve ½-inch white snowflake buttons or ¼-inch white buttons • Black 50-weight cotton thread • White 12- or 30-weight cotton thread • 18×24-inch piece batting

WHAT YOU DO

Preparing Background and Binding

1. Following the directions on the oval template on page 46, trace oval on stabilizer. Cut out ¼ inch beyond traced line.

2. Cut background/backing fabric in half. Pin oval to one piece of fabric and cut out around the oval.

3. Cut the binding fat quarter in half on the diagonal. On this bias cut four 2¼-inch strips for binding. See illustration, below, for cutting bias binding.

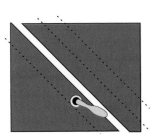

Cutting Bias Binding

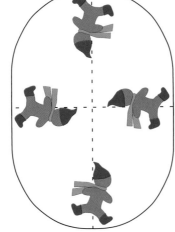

Positional Layout

Preparing Appliqué

1. Using the appliqué patterns on page 47 and tracing like pieces in groups on paper side of fusible web, trace four gingerbread men, four sets of boots, four hats, and four sets of scarves. Patterns are reversed.

2. Cut excess fusible web from around groups. Fuse according to manufacturer's directions to the corresponding fabrics listed in materials. Cut out each piece on the traced line.

Arranging and Stitching Appliqué

1. Remove the paper backing just before you arrange the appliqué.

2. Arrange each gingerbread man separately on a nonstick pressing sheet. If desired, enlarge and place the full-size layout, shown left, under the pressing sheet as a guide. Make four.

3. Arrange the gingerbread men on the background with the right boot about ¾ inch from the edge of the oval and the left edge of the hat on the center line.

4. Place the stabilizer under the background. Using matching thread and a satin or fine zigzag stitch (1mm long and 1.75mm wide), stitch around the appliqué pieces.

5. Use heavyweight white thread to decorate gingerbread men: Decorate the top of the boots and the brim of the hat with a snowball stitch, the cuffs with a triple stitch, and the ends of the scarves with a blanket stitch.

6. Referring to the layout illustration, page 47, mark the skate placements lightly with a pencil. With black thread and a triple stitch, stitch the skates.

Finishing

1. Layer the quilt top, batting, and backing.

2. Quilt as desired.

3. Trim the excess batting and backing to the oval.

4. Join the bias binding strips, fold in half, and use to bind quilt.

5. Sew on buttons to decorate the gingerbread men.

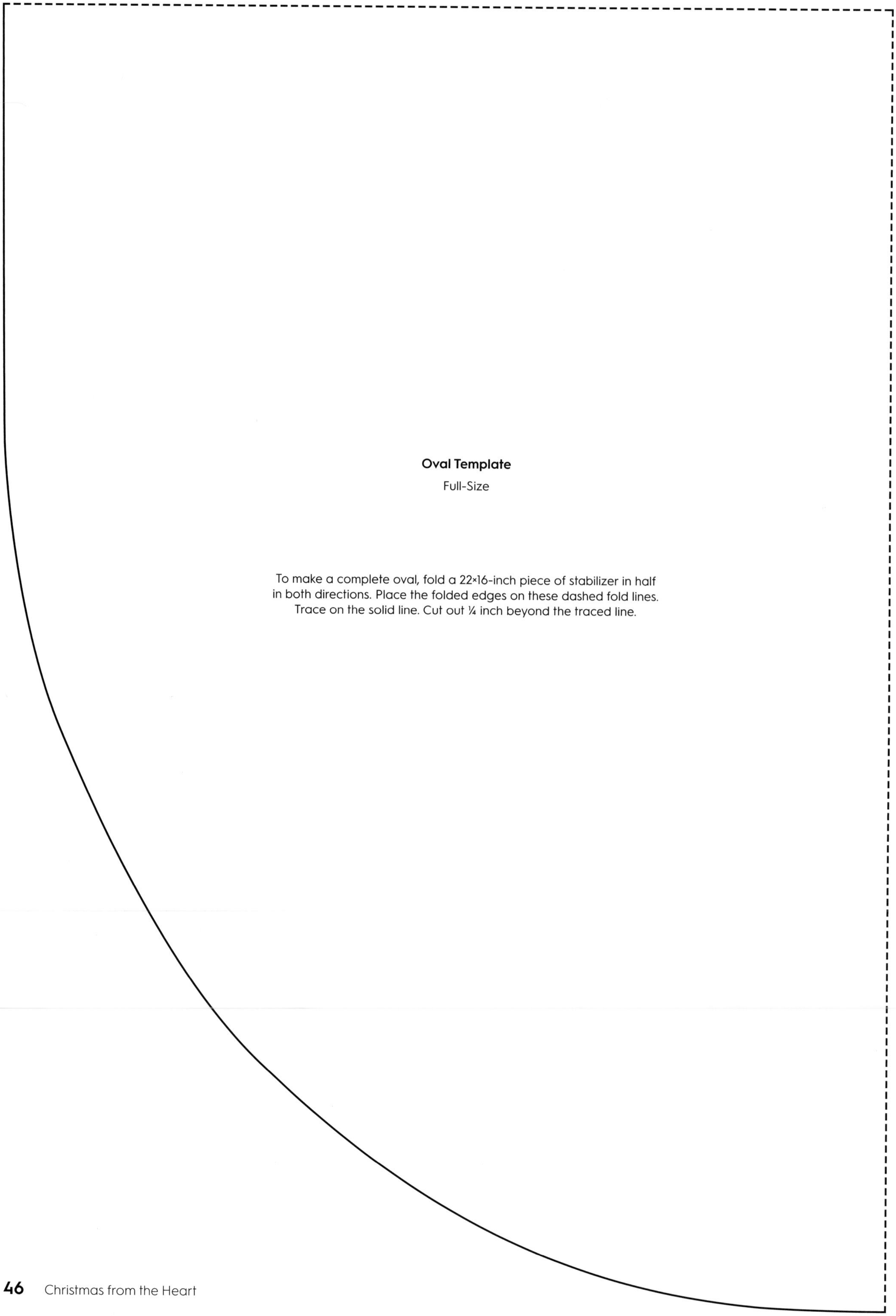

Oval Template

Full-Size

To make a complete oval, fold a 22×16-inch piece of stabilizer in half in both directions. Place the folded edges on these dashed fold lines. Trace on the solid line. Cut out ¼ inch beyond the traced line.

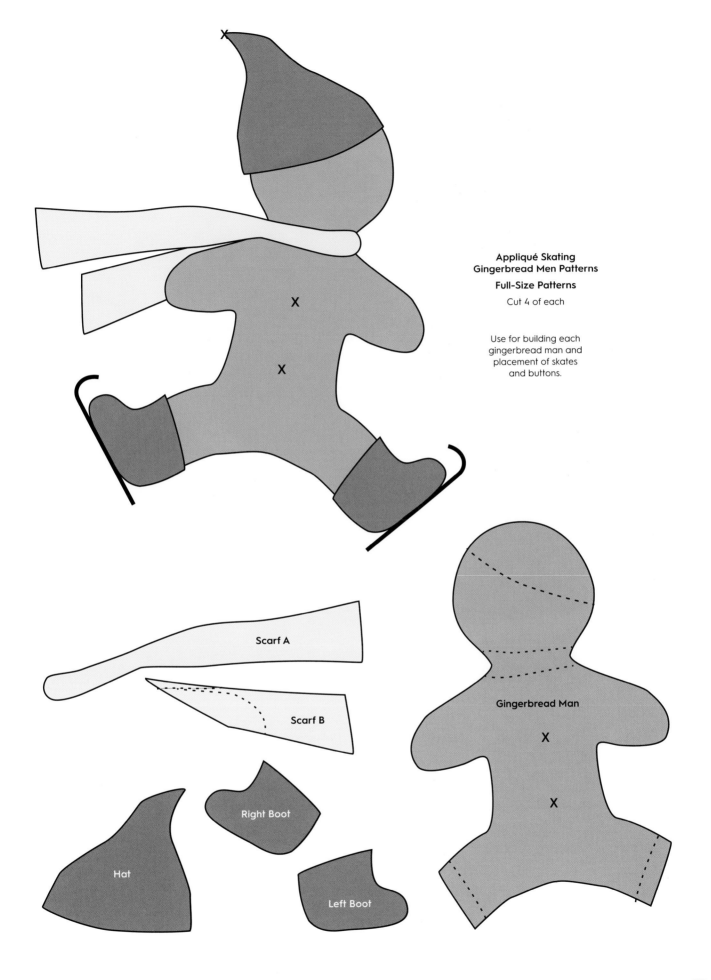

X

**Appliqué Skating
Gingerbread Men Patterns**

Full-Size Patterns

Cut 4 of each

Use for building each
gingerbread man and
placement of skates
and buttons.

X

X

Scarf A

Scarf B

Gingerbread Man

X

X

Hat

Right Boot

Left Boot

CATCH-ME-IF-YOU-CAN GINGERBREAD BOYS

Little felt gingerbread boys happily hold tiny treasures to share at Christmastime.

WHAT YOU NEED

Tracing paper • Pencil • Scissors • Gingerbread-color felt such as National Nonwovens • Cream-color embroidery floss • Needle • Thread to match body felt color • Polyester fiberfill • Embellishments such as buttons and heavyweight stickers • Fine cording

WHAT YOU DO

1. Trace pattern, opposite, and cut out. Trace onto felt, cutting two pieces for each gingerbread boy.

2. Using embroidery floss, embroider embellishments on the shape using desired embroidery stitches. See page 160 for stitch ideas and instructions.

3. With wrong sides together use matching thread to whipstitch around the edges of the felt, leaving a 1-inch opening on one side for stuffing. Lightly stuff the piece, leaving the arms unstuffed. Sew the side closed.

4. Bend the arms in and press. Sew a button or other embellishment between the hands. Add a fine cord for hanging.

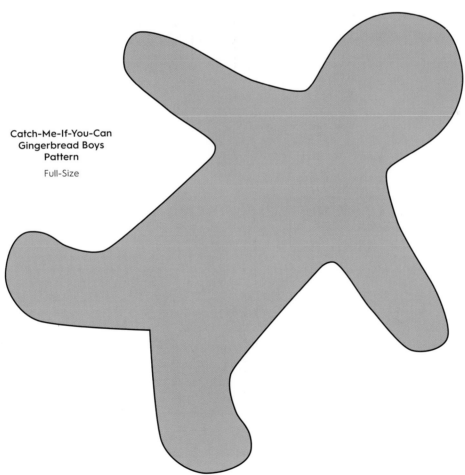

**Catch-Me-If-You-Can
Gingerbread Boys
Pattern**

Full-Size

SWEET GINGERBREAD HOUSES

Felt, floss, and clever embellishments combine to make these little gingerbread houses to hang on your kid-friendly Christmas tree.

WHAT YOU NEED

Tracing paper • Pencil • Scissors • Gingerbread-color felt such as National Nonwovens • Scraps of felt in white, red, and green • Tiny buttons and beads for embellishments • Embroidery floss in desired colors • Needle • Polyester fiberfill • Fine cording

WHAT YOU DO

1. Trace patterns, page 52, and cut out. Trace desired house shape onto felt, cutting two pieces for each house.

2. Cut snow-top shapes, roof shapes, pillar shapes, chimney tops, trees, and other desired trims from desired felt colors. With wrong sides together and using embroidery floss, use the buttonhole stitch to secure the embellishments in place. Referring to the photos for ideas, add beads, buttons, or other embellishments to the front of the house. See page 160 for embroidery stitch diagrams.

3. Place front and back of house with wrong sides together. Use matching embroidery floss and the buttonhole stitch to sew the pieces together, leaving a 1-inch opening on one side for stuffing. For the houses with chimneys, use the buttonhole stitch along the top edge of the roof. Lightly stuff the houses but do not stuff the chimneys. Stitch along chimney edge on house to remain flat. Sew the side closed.

4. Add a fine cord at the top for hanging.

Sweet Gingerbread Houses Patterns

Full-Size Patterns

ALL-IN-PINK GINGERBREAD TRIMS

Unexpected colors of paint dress up these flirty gingerbread people for a fun and festive tree trim.

WHAT YOU NEED

• Tracing paper • Pencil • Balsa wood, 1/32-inch thickness
• Crafts knife such as X-acto & cutting mat • Hole punch •
Crafts paint in desired colors • Painters tape • Fine string

WHAT YOU DO

1. Enlarge and copy the template, right. Using the template as a guide, cut shapes out of balsa using the crafts knife. Create a hole to hang the ornament using a hole punch.
2. To paint, apply painters tape down the center. Paint, let dry, and remove the tape. Attach string through hole.

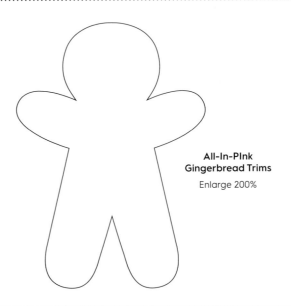

**All-In-PInk
Gingerbread Trims**

Enlarge 200%

GINGERBREAD BOY TIED PACKAGES

Decorate favorite gifts with a simple little gingerbread boy all tied up in strings.

WHAT YOU NEED

Tracing paper • Pencil • Scissors • Heavyweight cardstock in kraft brown • Scraps of wrapping paper • Paper punch • Bakers twine in desired color • Wrapped package in coordinating paper

WHAT YOU DO

1. Copy the template, right, and cut out. Trace around the shape onto cardstock and cut out. Punch a hole in each hand of the gingerbread shape.

2. Use scraps of wrapping paper to add details such as clothing to the shape.

3. Thread the cording through the holes and bring up to the front of the wrapped package and tie a bow.

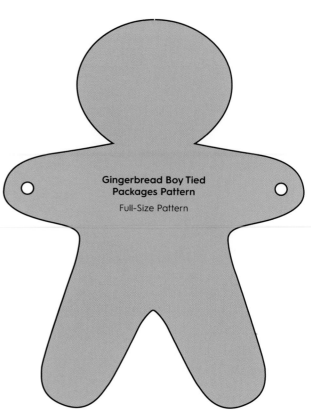

Gingerbread Boy Tied Packages Pattern

Full-Size Pattern

QUICK-TO-STAMP WRAPPING PAPER

Little gingerbread boys line up on kraft paper to make simple but adorable wraps for special gifts.

WHAT YOU NEED

Tracing paper • Pencil • Scissors • Hole punch • Spray adhesive • Craft foam • Block of wood • Crafts paint • Foam brush • Blank paper/wrapping paper • Red adhesive jewels

WHAT YOU DO

1. To make the stamp, copy the template, right. Trace around template onto a piece of crafts foam. Use the hole punch to create the buttons on the gingerbread man. Use spray adhesive to attach the crafts foam to the wooden block. Let dry.

2. When dry, apply crafts paint to the stamp using a foam brush, using just enough to cover the stamp. Practice stamping on scratch paper and then stamp on wrapping paper. Let dry.

3. Wrap gift as desired, adding red adhesive jewels to some of the button areas.

**Quick-to-Stamp
Wrapping Paper Pattern**

Full-Size Pattern

You are what you eat
So eat something sweet!

GINGERBREAD BOY KITCHEN HELPER

Delight yourself or a friend with a merry pieced pot holder. Embroider the sweet saying onto piecing strips, add a ruffle to the pot holder pocket, and embroider details on the gingerbread boy appliqué.

WHAT YOU NEED

Tracing paper • Pencil • Scissors • ¼ yard red-and-green dot print fabric (pocket front, ruffle, binding) • ¼ yard print fabric (lining and pot holder back) • ⅛ yard insulated batting • 2½×9-inch piece green dot print fabric (pocket back) • 2¼×9-inch piece tan dot print fabric (pocket front) • Embroidery floss in brown and white • Embroidery needle • Fusible web • 4×5-inch piece each of solid brown fabric and white felt • Two ½-inch-diameter white buttons • 5×9-inch piece pink holiday novelty print fabric (pocket front) • Sewing thread in brown and white • 9-inch square red holiday novelty print fabric (backing) • 1½×6-inch piece red-and-white dot print fabric (hanging loop)

Finished size: 9-inch square
Yardages and cutting instructions are based on 42 inches of usable fabric width. Measurements include ¼-inch seam allowances. Sew with right sides together unless otherwise stated.

WHAT YOU DO

Preparing Background and Binding

Cut the pieces in the following order:

From red-and-green dot print, cut:
1—¾×9-inch strip
1—1¾×15-inch strip
1—2×9-inch pocket binding strip
1—2½×42-inch binding strip

From lining print, cut:
2—7×9-inch rectangles

From insulated batting, cut:
1—9-inch square
1—7×9-inch rectangle

1. Trace the word patterns, page 58, onto white paper. Using a light box or a sunny window, center and trace the words **You are what you eat** onto the 2½×9-inch green dot print strip. Trace the words **So eat something sweet!** onto the 2¼×9-inch tan dot print strip, positioning the bottom of the letters 1½ inches below the strip's top edge. Using backstitches and three strands of brown embroidery floss, stitch the words on each fabric strip.

2. Trace the Gingerbread Boy pattern, page 58, onto paper side of fusible web; cut around the shape. With the fusible side down, press the shape onto the wrong side of solid brown fabric. Peel off the paper backing and press the gingerbread

boy onto the white felt. Cut around the gingerbread boy, leaving a scant 1⁄16-inch white felt border. Referring to the pattern, satin-stitch the eyes and straight-stitch the face and frosting lines using six strands of white embroidery floss. Sew buttons to center front of gingerbread boy.

Assemble the Pot Holder Pocket

1. Referring to the Pot Holder Pocket Front Assembly Diagram, page 58, sew the ¾×9-inch red-and-green dot print strip to bottom long edge of the embroidered tan dot print strip. Sew the 5×9-inch pink holiday novelty print rectangle to the remaining long edge of the red-and-green dot print strip. Press seams toward the tan and pink rectangles.

2. Layer the pocket front atop a 7×9-inch lining print rectangle with the 7×9-inch insulated batting rectangle between the layers; baste.

3. Quilt the 5×9-inch pink holiday novelty print rectangle as desired through all layers.

4. Fold the 1¾×15-inch red-and-green dot print strip in half lengthwise with wrong sides together. Stitch a long running stitch ¼ inch from unfinished edges through both layers. Pull one thread end and gather the fabric to make a 9-inch-long ruffle. Sew the ruffle to the top edge of the pocket front (Diagram 1, page 58).

5. Topstitch the gingerbread boy on the right half of the pink holiday novelty print rectangle on pocket front using brown thread (Diagram 1, page 58).

6. With wrong side inside, fold 2×9-inch red-and-green dot print pocket binding strip in half lengthwise. With raw edges even, sew strip to lining side at top of pocket front. Bring folded edge to front and topstitch close to fold to bind top of pocket front.

Assemble the Pot Holder Back

1. Referring to the Pot Holder Back Assembly Diagram, page 58, sew the embroidered green dot print strip to remaining 7×9-inch lining print rectangle for pot holder back.

2. Layer the pot holder back atop the 9-inch red holiday novelty print backing square with the 9-inch square of insulated batting between the layers; baste. Quilt the pot holder back as desired. Note: We stitched horizontal lines across the pot holder back, spacing them 1½ inches apart.

3. Place the pot holder pocket atop the pot holder back, aligning bottom and side edges. Baste sides and bottom.

4. With wrong side inside, fold 1½×6-inch red-and-white dot print strip in half lengthwise. Lightly press, then unfold. Fold long raw edges in to meet at center. Refold strip in half lengthwise, aligning folded edges; press again. Edgestitch folded edges. Matching raw ends, fold strip in half to make a hanging loop; baste loop to pot holder back.

5. Bind the pot holder with the 2½×42-inch red-and-green dot print binding strip, mitering corners as you go.

Diagram 1

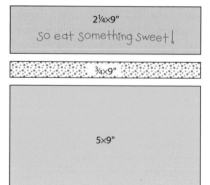

2¼×9"
So eat something sweet!

¾×9"

5×9"

Pot Holder Pocket Front
Assembly Diagram

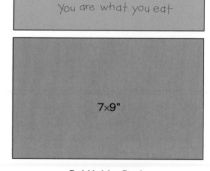

2½×9"
You are what you eat

7×9"

Pot Holder Back
Assembly Diagram

So eat something Sweet!

You are what you eat

Gingerbread Boy
Kitchen Helper Patterns
Full-Size

Gingerbread Boy

HOLDING-HANDS GARLAND

All-dressed-up paper gingerbread boys stand together linked with red-and-white bakers twine for a quick-to-make garland.

WHAT YOU NEED
Tracing paper • Pencil • Scissors • Brown cardstock • Paper punch • White and red dimensional paint in a tube • Red-and-white bakers twine

WHAT YOU DO
1. Trace the template, right, and cut out. Trace around the shape onto cardstock and cut out. Cut as many as desired. Punch a hole in each hand of each gingerbread shape.
2. Use dimensional paint to make designs on the shapes, referring to the photo for inspiration.
3. Thread the bakers twine through the holes to connect for a garland.

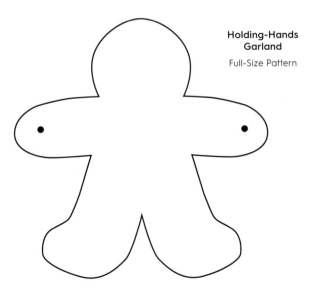

Holding-Hands Garland

Full-Size Pattern

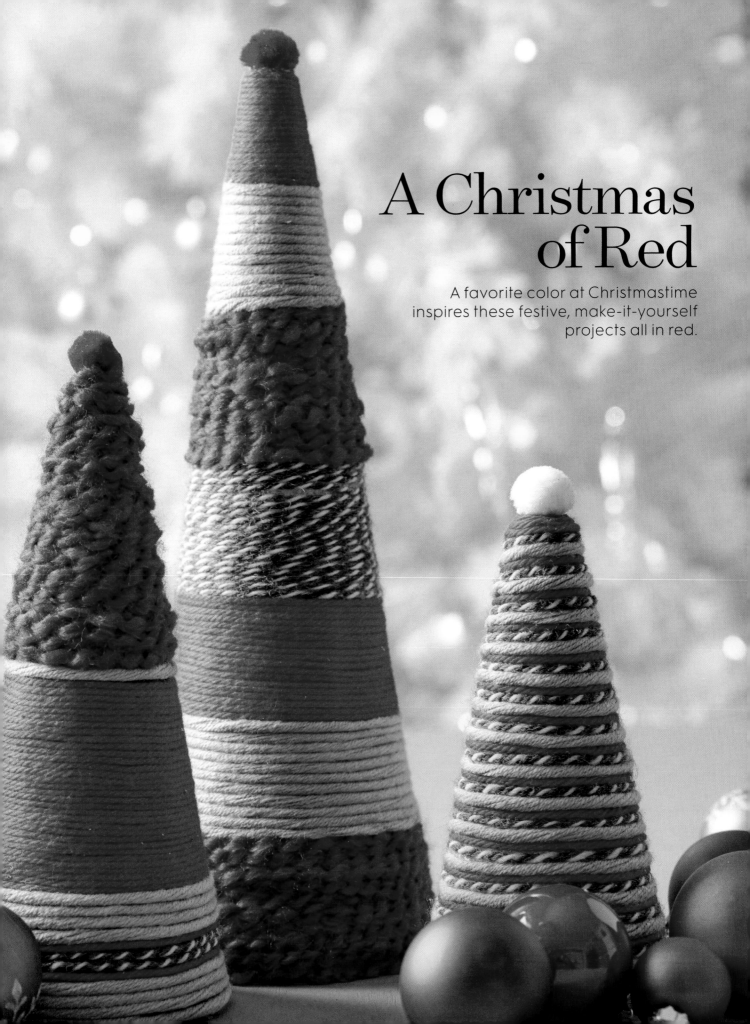

A Christmas of Red

A favorite color at Christmastime inspires these festive, make-it-yourself projects all in red.

CRANBERRY-RED CANDLE CENTERPIECE

WHAT YOU NEED

2 clear tumbler glasses • Florists putty • Red taper candles • Fresh cranberries • Glass tray • Fresh greenery and holly

WHAT YOU DO

1. Be sure the glasses are clean and dry. Center putty in the bottom of each glass. Push the candles into the putty to secure.
2. Arrange the cranberries around the candles. Set the glasses on a glass tray and add greenery and holly.

HERBS AND POMEGRANATE DISPLAY

Use grocery-store produce that is timely at Christmastime to make a stunning centerpiece. Start with a red tray or dish and add a red candle. Then surround the candle with pomegranates, cut and whole, for texture and color. Tuck in a few fresh herbs such as sage and rosemary for a last-minute touch.

TRIO OF TREES

Yarn, cording, and pom-poms in shades of red blend with a bit of neutral gray to make a set of trees for your holiday mantel.

WHAT YOU NEED

3 foam cone forms such as Styrofoam in varying heights • Yarn and cording in shades of red and gray in various weights and styles • Crafts glue • Paintbrush • Short straight pins • Pom-poms

WHAT YOU DO

1. Plan the design of the trees. Starting at the top, wind the yarn or cording around the foam cone using a little crafts glue with a paintbrush to keep yarn or cording in place. Use pins to secure at beginning and end.

2. Continue adding the yarn and cording until desired design is completed.

3. Add pom-poms at the top of each tree using crafts glue or pins.

CHRISTMAS-RED CROCHET HAT
Celebrate the season with a holiday hat crocheted in red.

WHAT YOU NEED
No. 4 medium-weight red yarn • Size K crochet hook •
Button • Needle

Crochet Abbreviations are on page 160.

WHAT YOU DO

FOR THE HAT BODY:
Use magic circle or ch 6 to start, join w/sl st, 10 sc in circle,
ch 1. Do not turn. Ch 1, 10 sts.
Row 1: 2 hdc in each sc around, join w/sl st in first st of the row,
ch 1, 20 sts.
Row 2: 2 hdc in every other st around 1 hdc in the other sts. Join
w/sl st, ch 1, 30 sts.
Row 3: 2 hdc in first st, 1 hdc in next 2 sts. Repeat round. Join w/
sl st ch 1, 40 sts.
Row 4: 2 hdc in first st, 1 hdc in each of next 3 sts. Repeat
around. Join w/ sl st, ch 1, 50 sts.
Row 5: 2 hdc in first st, 1 hdc in next 4 sts. Repeat around. Join w/
st st, ch 1, 60 sts.
Row 6: 2 hdc in first st, 1 hdc in each of next 5 sts. Repeat
around. Join w/sl st, ch 1, 70 st.
Row 7: Work even hdc for next 10 rows or desired length to fit.
End off and weave end in.

FOR THE HAT BAND:
On the inside of the hat, find the 20th st to the right of center.
Join and sc in each st around only in the back loop of the stitch.
When you get around to the first st, ch 7-10 depending how
long you want the overlap. Sc in the second chain in back loop
only. Continue back around to the end. This will make a rib
stitch. Ch 1, turn. Repeat rows of rib stitch until desired length,
ending with an inside row. Continue around. When you get to
the overlap, turn corners by adding an inc. in each corner.
Sc in end st of overlap, inc in corner, sc on overlap to where it
joins the band. Finish off. Sew a button at the flap. **Note:** You
can stitch the flap down to make it more secure.

CHRISTMASTIME PACKAGE TAG

Transform a plain white box into a noteworthy present by dressing it with a plush velvet ribbon tied in a blousy bow and a birds-in-a-tree gift tag. To dress the wrapping, adhere scallop-edge paper trim along the folded paper edge.

WHAT YOU NEED

Purchased tree stamp • Black ink stamp pad • White cardstock • Red and black fine-tip markers • Patterned and red scrapbook papers • Double-stick foam circles such as Pop Dot • ⅛-inch-wide red ribbon

WHAT YOU DO

1. Using the tree stamp, stamp a tree shape on the white paper. Cut out a rectangle with tree in center.

2. Use the red marker to draw tiny birds on tree stamp and the black marker to color in the tree if needed.

3. Cut out a larger rectangle from red paper and an even larger one from patterned paper. Use foam circles to connect the tag's three paper layers. Loop length of ribbon and glue to card.

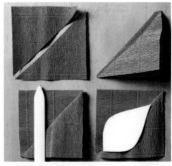

CREPE-PAPER GIFT TOPPER

Layers of heavyweight crepe paper create bracts with plenty of body. A dusting of glitter makes these toppers glisten with the season.

WHAT YOU NEED

Heavy crepe paper • Rotary cutter and mat • Crafts glue • Bone folder • Bract templates • Gold glitter glue • Flat or sponge paintbrush • Hot-glue gun and glue sticks • Glass glitter • Double-stick tape

WHAT YOU DO

1. Cut eighteen 5-inch squares from crepe paper. Cut each in half on the diagonal. Stack two triangles together so the crepe paper grain aligns. Apply a bead of crafts glue to bind the long edges of triangles. Set aside to dry. Repeat for remaining 17 pairs.

2. Open the triangles and flatten the center with the bone folder. The textured lines should move in opposite directions like the veins of a bract. Enlarge and trace the templates, right. Centering templates on the creases, trace six each large (4¾ inches long), medium (4¼ inches long), and small

(3¼ inches long) bracts. Cut out. Outline each with a bead of glitter glue. Use brush to pull glitter glue toward center of bract. Let dry.

3. Fan the large bracts in a circle. Secure bracts with a dot of hot glue between each. Layer the medium bracts on top, staggering them between the large bracts; glue. Add a layer of small bracts. Apply a dot of hot glue to the center and sprinkle with glass glitter. Let dry. Attach to gift with double-stick tape.

Crepe-Paper Gift Topper Bract Templates

Enlarge 300%

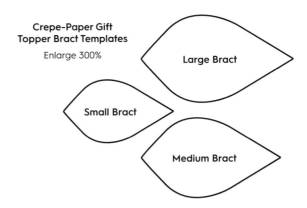

Large Bract

Small Bract

Medium Bract

ALL-IN-RED CHRISTMAS TABLE SETTING

Your table will shine with the spirit of the season when you use red as your color scheme. Start with a red place mat and then layer a red charger, a red napkin, and a recycled Christmas card. Finish with a clear glass plate and a simple candy and berry topper. Add candles in a small dish with gold tinsel and gold flatware to add to the stunning presentation.

From light pink and fuchsia to Christmas red and burgundy, shades of red line up on a foam cone shape to make a stunning little tree for a mantel or simple centerpiece.

OMBRE RED MINI TREE
Felt balls in lovely shades of red stack up to make a one-of-a-kind tree topped off with a flowing ribbon.

WHAT YOU NEED
Felt balls in shades of red (see Sources, page 160) • 6-inch plastic foam tree form such as Styrofoam • Hot-glue gun and glue sticks • ⅜-inch ribbon in shade of red

WHAT YOU DO
1. Plan the design by laying out the balls in color groups from light to dark. Working in small areas at a time, hot-glue the balls to the cone, starting at the bottom using the darker balls first, and ending with the lighter balls at the top. Let dry.
2. Tie a bow with the ribbon and hot-glue the bow at the top of the tree, letting the tails drape down.

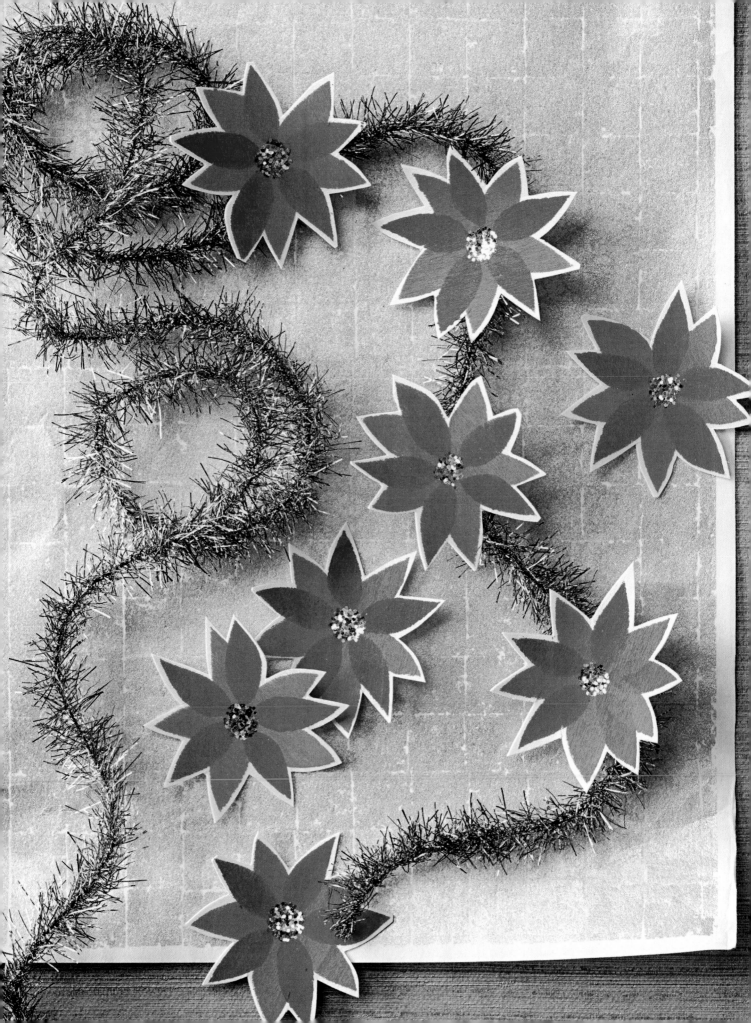

POINSETTIA BLOOM TINSEL GARLAND

Create a glittery accent for your tree, green garland, or holiday table centerpiece using a tinsel garland peppered with poinsettia blooms you've crafted from thin veneer.

WHAT YOU NEED

Tracing paper • Pencil • White cardstock • Crafts knife or scissors • Stencil brush • Acrylic paint in various reds • Thin crafting wood veneer sheet • Glitter glue • Silver glitter • Thin gold tinsel garland

WHAT YOU DO

1. Trace the petal stencil template, below, onto cardstock. Cut out the inside of the petal shape to create a stencil.
2. Lightly dip the brush into paint. Dab the brush on a paper towel until the brush is almost dry. Stencil five petals onto the wood veneer sheet. Let dry. Repeat with a different red paint, placing new petals between existing stenciled petals to form a larger flower. **Note:** The different shades of red will give a dimensional effect.
3. Dab glue in center; dust with glitter. Cut out flower, leaving veneer edge of wood showing on flower.
4. Repeat to create enough flowers for the garland. Attach flowers to purchased tinsel garland with glue.

Cut out inside shape

**Poinsettia Bloom
Tinsel Garland Stencil
Template**

Full-Size Stencil Pattern

Make a major statement with an ombré tannenbaum that is sure to be the center of attention. This 9-foot stunner showcases nine graduations of red from tip to trunk. Glass ball ornaments and wired ribbons in varying sizes and sheens set the tree aglow.

COLOR-CASCADE OMBRÉ TREE

Choose ball ornaments in all sizes and shades of red to make this stunning tree for your holiday home.

WHAT YOU NEED

Prelit artificial tree in desired height • Ribbons with similar weight, width, and style in desired shades of red • Multiple sizes of glass or plastic ball ornaments in both matte and shiny finishes in desired shades of red • Ornament hooks or other hangers such as small ribbons • Scissors

WHAT YOU DO

1. Plan the tree by gathering ornaments from lightest to darkest. You'll need fewer at the top than the bottom so you'll need more dark-hue ornaments than light.

2. Choose ribbons with similar weight, width, and style in your chosen shades. Wired satin ribbon is a good choice because it retains its shape. **Note:** The bottom of the tree will require more ribbon than the top.

3. Continue the color palette with multiple sizes of glass or plastic ball ornaments in both matte and shiny finishes. Decorate the tree from the inside out, hanging ornaments from the trunk to the branch tops. Tie ribbons on the outside branches of the tree.

CUSTOM-COLOR ORNAMENTS

Swirl acrylic paint in shades of red inside clear glass balls. Then scatter snowy stickers around the balls' exteriors and show off your tailor-made spheres in a clear bowl.

WHAT YOU NEED

Clear-glass ball ornaments • Muffin pan • Plastic wrap • Acrylic paints in multiple shades of red acrylic paint • Snowflake stickers

WHAT YOU DO

1. Remove hangers and caps from ornaments; set aside. Line muffin cups with plastic wrap; set aside.

2. Choose paint colors and add a few drops of water to each paint color. Squirt a single paint color into each ornament. Swirl until paint covers the inside.

3. Place ornaments upside down in lined muffin cups so excess paint can drop into cups. Let dry overnight. If needed, swirl additional paint inside balls; let dry. Reattach caps and hangers. Adhere snowflake stickers to the exteriors.

SHIFT SHADES

Swirling orbs that begin as papier-mâché shapes take on a classic beauty when covered in patterned paper. Beads and ball-head pins finish the tips with appropriate holiday glitz.

WHAT YOU NEED

Six-sided papier-mâché ornament • Scrapbook paper • Scratch paper • Crafts glue • Glossy acrylic varnish • Paintbrush • ⅛-inch-wide red ribbon • Red beads • White ball-head pin

WHAT YOU DO

1. Lay the ornament on the wrong side of the scrapbook paper. Trace a panel six times, leaving space between the tracings. Cut out three paper panels, cutting on the traced lines.

2. Around the remaining three traced panels, draw a line ¼ inch away for a seam allowance. Cut out the remaining paper panels, cutting on the seam allowance line. Clip into seam allowances, and glue those paper panels to the ornament on alternating sides, smoothing seam allowances over ridges.

3. Glue the remaining paper panels in place, covering the seam allowances of the already glued paper panels. Let glue dry. Seal all surfaces with glossy varnish. Let dry. Attach a looped ribbon to the ornament top with a red bead and ball-head pin. Attach a red bead to the ornament bottom with a ball-head pin.

WRAPPED IN RED

'Tis more fun to give than to receive when you take the time to make each package its own work of art. Try your hand at these masterpieces.

Very Merry

Star-Crossed

Ho Ho Ho

VERY MERRY

Pick the same ribbon in three colors for a simple, layered look. We used linen ribbons in Christmas red, pink, and moss green.

STAR-CROSSED

Crisscrossed ribbons and a star-shape ornament mark this gift as extra special.

HO HO HO

Packing tape secures sequins to ordinary gift wrap. Seasonal washi tape adds playful patterns.

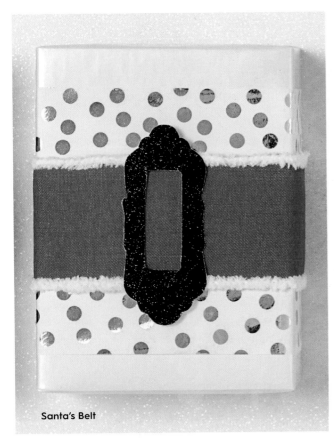

Santa's Belt

Snowflake Trimmed

SANTA'S BELT

A novelty ribbon plays dress-up as Santa's belt when embellished with a DIY paper buckle.

SNOWFLAKE TRIMMED

Mix novelty trim, such as these dancing snowflakes, with more traditional ribbon to add a level of textural interest.

TINSEL LEFTOVERS

Clippings from larger decorations, like this pouf made from a small piece of a tinsel garland, give you more bang for your buck.

Tinsel Leftovers

Love to Give

Handmade gifts are the best gifts of all! So find your special talent and share it with the ones you love by presenting a gift you've created just for them.

Softly Scented
Sachets
Embroidering
Diagrams

SOFTLY SCENTED SACHETS

*Bits of soft wool, scraps from a recycled sweater, a
favorite fragrance, and simple stitches combine to make
lovely sachets to share.*

WHAT YOU NEED

Small pieces of white wool • Small pieces of colored wool or
felted wool made from a recycled sweater • Scissors
• Thread to match fabrics • Polyester fiberfill • Fresh
balsam, lavender, thyme, or essential oils in desired
fragrance on a small piece of cotton • Cream embroidery
floss • Pearl beads • Embroidery needle

WHAT YOU DO

1. Cut a piece of white wool and a piece of colored wool each
into a 3×3-inch square. With right sides together, stitch around
the square using a ⅜-inch seam, leaving a 1-inch opening for
turning. Trim corners and turn right side out. Press.
2. Stuff lightly with polyester fiberfill. Add desired scent. Stitch
opening closed.
3. Referring to the diagrams, above, embroider simple lines on
the sachet fronts, adding pearl beads into the design.

For the wrap

Place sachets in small kraft box. Tie with brown string, small
ornaments, and herbs such as lavender and thyme.

TOO-CUTE POM-POM EARRINGS

Tiny pom-poms line up on gold earring hoops to make a sweet little gift for Christmas.

WHAT YOU NEED

Two 28 mm teardrop earring hoops • 2 fish-hook ear wires • Two 6mm round split rings • Mini pom-poms • Needle-nose pliers • Hot-glue gun and glue sticks

WHAT YOU DO

1. Using needle-nose pliers, separate the wires of the split rings and attach one fish-hook ear wire and one teardrop hoop like putting keys on a keychain.

2. Attach mini pom-poms to the ends of the teardrop hoops or to the round split rings with hot glue.

For the wrap

Use a gold marking pen to write "for you" around the lip of the lid of the box. Tie with gold ribbon.

KITCHEN HELPERS SPOONS AND PLACE MAT

Purchased wooden spoons are wrapped with bright fabrics for a fun kitchen set that anyone would love.

WHAT YOU NEED

Wooden spoons ● Fabric in desired color and design (one fat quarter makes one spoon/place mat) ● Decoupage medium such as Mod Podge ● Foam brush ● Ribbon to coordinate with fabric ● Gift tag ● Alphabet stamps and ink stamp pad ● Fine-tip marker

WHAT YOU DO

1. Cut a small strip of fabric large enough to wrap around base of spoon once. Attach to wooden spoon by applying a thin layer of decoupage medium onto the spoon handle. When fabric is attached, apply another thin layer of decoupage medium on top of the fabric to seal. Let dry.

2. Fray the edges of a 12×18-inch piece of remaining fabric to create a decorative place mat. Fold and press to make a folded piece about 4×6 inches.

3. To make the tag, glue a scrap of the fabric to the tag and stamp a name on the tag. To present the gift, lay the spoon on the folded place mat, tie a ribbon around the spoon, and add the tag.

PAINTED TEA SET

Plain white ceramic kitchen accessories are inexpensive, readily available, and perfect for embellishing with paint pens or permanent markers.

WHAT YOU NEED

Purchased white ceramic item to decorate • Paint pens suitable for ceramic or permanent markers such as Sharpie • White paper • Transfer paper if using patterns • Pencil

WHAT YOU DO

1. Freehand your design on the ceramic piece, or choose a pattern you like and trace onto white paper and cut around the outside of the pattern. Cut a piece of transfer paper slightly larger than the area to be doodled, and tape it to the surface. Tape the pattern over the transfer paper.

2. Using a pencil, firmly trace the pattern lines to transfer the design to the surface. Remove the pattern and the transfer paper.

3. Using a paint pen or permanent marker, trace the lines; let dry. Cure the paint by baking the piece in the oven following the manufacturer's instructions. **Note:** Hand-wash pieces only.

SWEET AND SIMPLE SWEATER HAT

Recycle a favorite sweater into a sweet little hat that you can make in an evening and give the next day.

WHAT YOU NEED

Tracing paper • Pencil • Castaway wool sweater with ribbing at bottom • Thread to match sweater color • Scissors • Small piece of contrasting wool for flower • Contrasting thread for wool flower • Small button

WHAT YOU DO

1. Referring to the template, right, enlarge and make a pattern adjusting to fit the size of head to fit.

2. Plan where the pattern pieces are to be cut from the sweater. Flatten the sweater, cutting as necessary, and laying the pattern pieces so the bottom of the hat is on the bottom ribbing of the sweater. Cut out a front and back for the hat.

3. With right sides together, pin the front and back together and stitch using a ⅜-inch seam. Turn and press.

4. To make the flower, refer to the pattern, right, and cut two flower shapes and one center shape from wool. Topstitch around the flower shapes for decorative color. Layer the flower shapes and sew the small circle on top. Place the button on top of the layers, and stitch through the layers onto the hat.

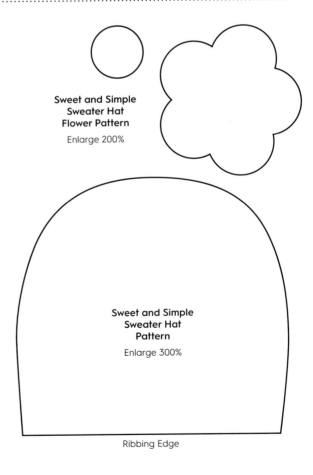

Sweet and Simple Sweater Hat Flower Pattern

Enlarge 200%

Sweet and Simple Sweater Hat Pattern

Enlarge 300%

Ribbing Edge

MASON JAR COASTER SET

With just a little fun-color cording, glue, and Mason jar lids, you can create a clever coaster set and all the goodies to go with it!

WHAT YOU NEED

Wide-mouth Mason jar lids • Fine sandpaper • Hot-glue gun and glue sticks • Twine in desired colors • Crafts glue

WHAT YOU DO

1. Plan the design of the coaster. The twine can be glued around the edge of the jar lid or directly on the jar lid flat.
2. Lightly sand the area to be glued. Apply the twine with a dab of hot glue at the beginning and end, and using crafts glue as needed. When gluing to the jar flat, use a spiral pattern starting at the middle of the circle. Trim off ends.
3. To make the gift, fill two small Mason jars: one with hot chocolate mix and one with mini marshmallows. Label the jars, tie a ribbon around the top, and add the finished coasters.

SPECS CASE

Whether you delve into your ribbon scraps or pick and choose the perfect coordinating ribbons, this eyeglass case is easy to make using fusible webbing and a flannel backing. Machine-embroidered decorative stitches dress up the ribbon edges.

WHAT YOU NEED

7-inch square fusible webbing • 7-inch square flannel • Assorted ribbon cut into 7-inch lengths

WHAT YOU DO

1. Place fusible-web square on top of flannel square. Arrange ribbon on the fusible webbing, positioning the ribbon close together. Position the ribbon along the top edge of the square so it extends ¼ inch beyond the webbing. Following the manufacturer's instructions for the fusible webbing, fuse ribbon to the flannel square.

2. Machine-stitch along the long ribbon edges using a variety of decorative stitches. Fold the ribbon along the top edge to the back and topstitch close to the edge.

3. Fold the piece with right sides together, aligning the ribbon ends. Sew the long edge and the bottom short edge using a ¼-inch seam allowance and round the corner. Clip the corner; turn the case right side out and press.

BEACHY SOAPS AND LOOFA CLOTH

A quick-to-crochet loofa cloth and some handmade soaps studded with shells becomes the perfect gift for the beach-lover on your Christmas list.

WHAT YOU NEED

FOR THE LOOFA BATH SCRUBBIE
Finished size of cloth is approximately 8×10 inches
K size hook • One 3 oz. skein Red Heart size 4 100% cotton Scrubby yarn in desired color

Crochet Abbreviations are on page 160.

FOR THE BEACHY SOAPS
Glycerin soap such as Neutrogena or purchased glycerin soap cubes • Glass measuring cup • Small shells • Molds such as muffin cups or purchased soap molds • Microwave • Toothpick

WHAT YOU DO

FOR THE LOOFA BATH SCRUBBIE
Chain 33 sts.
Sc in second chain from hook and the remaining ch sts.
Ch 2 and turn, 32 stitches.
Row 1: Dc in each sc across row, ch 1 and turn.
Row 2: Sc in each st across row, ch 2 and turn.
Alternate Row 1 and Row 2 to create the pattern. Repeat 10 times or to desired length. End with Row 1. Sc around edge to finish. Increase 2 in corner st to turn the corner.
Finish off with a sl st, and conceal the tail.

FOR THE BEACHY SOAPS
1. Cube purchased soap or use soap cubes and place in glass measuring cup. Set aside.
2. Prepare molds by placing a small shell in each mold.
3. Place measuring cup in microwave and heat until just melted. Do not overheat.
4. Pour melted soap into the molds. As the soap hardens, use a toothpick to gently push the shell into the middle of the mold. Let soap harden completely.
5. Remove soap from mold.

EASY PATCHWORK POT HOLDERS

Choose a quilters' charm pack in a pattern that suits you and whip up some pot holders for quick and easy gifts.

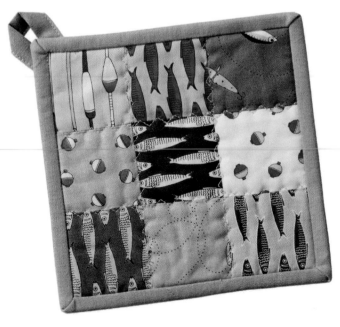

WHAT YOU NEED

Nine 2½-inch squares or charm pack squares • Two 9-inch squares of insulated batting such as Insulbrite • 9-inch square fabric for backing • 2¼-inch-wide strips fabric for binding, or bias tape • Spray adhesive

WHAT YOU DO

1. Arrange the nine squares into desired design. Using ¼-inch seam, stitch together. Press seams open.
2. Layer the backing, insulated batting, and the nine-patch top, using adhesive to hold in place. Quilt in desired pattern.
3. Square up the pot holder to a 6½-inch square.
4. Prepare binding and stitch in place, turning corners and joining ends using your favorite method. Make a 4- to 5-inch fabric strip stitched together to use as a hanger. Attach to a corner; pull binding to back and stitch in place.

SIMPLY KNITTED MITTENS

Keep out the cold with these simple mittens—perfect for everyone on your Christmas list. So easy to knit, the finished mitten can be either right or left hand.

WHAT YOU NEED

Worsted weight #3 yarn in desired color • Circular needles in size #6 and #8 • Needle

WHAT YOU DO

Knitting Abbreviations are on page 160.

Cast on: 40 (S), 42 (M), 44 (L)

CUFF RIBBING PATTERN

k2, p2 repeat across row. Work in even pattern until cuff measures 1.5" (2.0", 2.5")
Change to #8 circular needles

BODY

Work in stockinette stitch; Next 4(S), 6(M), 8(L) rows

THUMB SHAPING (FOR ALL SIZES)

Increase Knit 19 (21, 23) M1, k2, M1, k19 (21, 23).
Purl next row.
k19, (21, 23), M1, k4, M1, k19 (21, 23). Purl next row.
k19, (21, 23), M1, k6, M1, k19 (21, 23). Purl next row.
k19, (21, 23), M1, k8, M1, k19 (21, 23). Purl next row.
k19, (21, 23), M1, k10, M1, k19 (21, 23). Purl next row.

MEDIUM AND LARGE

k21, (23), M1, k12, M1, k21 (23). Purl row.

LARGE

k23, M1, k14, M1, k23. Purl row.
k19 (21, 23) put 12 (14, 16) on stitch holder
k19 (21, 23).
Knit the rest of the body in stockinette st until measures 7" (S) 7.5" (M) 8" (L)

MITTEN TOP SHAPING

k1, ssk, 13 (15, 17), k2tog, k2, ssk, k13 (15, 17), k2 tog, k1. Purl next row.
k1, ssk, k11 (13, 15), k2 tog, k2, ssk, k11 (13, 15), k2 tog, k1. Purl next row.
k1, ssk, k9 (11, 13), k2 tog, k2, ssk, k9 (11, 13), k2 tog, k1. Purl next row. k1, ssk, k7 (9, 11), k2 tog, k2, ssk, k7 (9, 11), k2 tog, k1. Purl next row. k1, ssk, k5 (7, 9), k2 tog, k2 ssk, s5 (7, 9), k2 tog, k1. Purl next row.
Knit off remaining sts. Leave long tail to use later to sew side seam together.

THUMB

Divide stitches evenly on dbl pointed needles. Knit in stockinette st until measures 2" (2.25", 2.5").

SHAPE TOP OF THUMB

Decrease evenly for all sizes.
k2, k2 tog, k2, k2 tog, k2, k2 tog.
Next round, decrease w/k1, k2 tog around. Leave 8" tail.
Using a yarn needle, thread w/the tail and draw through remaining sts. Secure and bury the end.
Use yarn tails and sew the side seam and tie off.

FINISHING: Make 2 mittens. Thread the needle with a long piece of yarn. Work a running stitch right under the ribbing, leaving tails to tie into a bow. Tie into a bow.

A Touch of Sparkle

Give your Christmas decorating the Midas touch with plenty of glitter, shimmer, and shine.

GLITTERING GARLAND

Leaf shapes cut from both plain and gold-leaf kraft paper gather along a length of rope to create a sumptuous garland that is at once sophisticated and warm.

WHAT YOU NEED

Tracing paper • Pencil • Scissors • Kraft paper, both plain and gold-leaf (directions on how to make gold-leaf kraft paper are below) • Hot-glue gun and glue sticks • Metallic decorative paper • 1-inch-thick rope • Florists wire • Christmas balls • Bell ornaments

WHAT YOU DO

1. Enlarge and copy the template, below. Trace and cut multiples of leaf pattern on all three kinds of paper. You will need about 50 cutouts for each foot of garland.
2. Gently fold each leaf down the center. Apply glue to stems and adhere stems to rope in layers, working all the way around the rope.
3. Hang the garland by draping it over nails or hooks attached to the wall or mantel. Use florists wire to attach balls and bell ornaments.

HOW TO MAKE GOLD-LEAF KRAFT PAPER

WHAT YOU NEED

Roll of kraft paper • Crafts glue • Two foam brushes • Sheets of gold leaf

WHAT YOU DO

Unroll a section of kraft paper on a flat surface. Brush on random, imperfect swaths of crafts glue with a foam brush. Do not coat entire surface with glue. Allow glue to set until tacky, then apply gold leaf sheets by gently rubbing in place with your finger. Remove gold leaf from unglued areas by gently dusting with the dry foam brush.

**Glittering Garland
Leaf Pattern**

Enlarge 200%

PAPER FLOWERS

Blossoms created from gold-leaf kraft paper are a holiday heavyweight. Snip a bunch of bloomers and attach to a fresh wreath or gold-painted branches.

WHAT YOU NEED

Tracing paper • Pencil • Scissors • Gold-leaf kraft paper (see page 93) • Crafts glue • Gold beads

WHAT YOU DO

1. Enlarge flower patterns, below. Cut flower shapes from gold-leaf kraft paper. Fold each in half along dotted lines as shown on pattern; unfold.
2. Fold in half along other axis; unfold. Glue a bead in center. Attach to a fresh wreath or glue to gold-painted branches.

Paper Flowers Patterns
Enlarge 125%

CIRCLE GARLAND

This sophisticated swag, made using paper spheres and beads, dresses up any holiday mantel, sideboard, or banister.

WHAT YOU NEED

Kraft paper, both plain and gold-leaf (see page 93) • Metallic decorative paper • 2-inch circle punch • Bone folder • Ribbon or string • Beads

WHAT YOU DO

1. Punch or cut out eight 2-inch circles in a variety of papers for each sphere you plan to make. (It takes about five spheres to make a foot of garland.) Use the bone folder to fold each circle in half.

2. Glue back side of one folded circle to back side of another folded circle. Before you glue the last two circle backs together, glue ribbon or string to the fold. Then glue last two circle backs together. Tie a bead to the string before beginning to make next sphere.

GOLDEN TREE AND TOPPER

Bold gold and minimal details keep this do-it-yourself tree topper from looking fussy. Made from kraft paper decked in gold leaf, the project is as simple as cutting, folding, and gluing. Add cut-paper holly leaves and golden pinecones to finish this glimmering tree.

WHAT YOU NEED

Tracing paper • Pencil • Scissors • Gold-leaf kraft paper (see page 93) • Paper • Crafts knife • Ruler• Dowel or heavy wire • Bone folder • Glue Stick • Tape

WHAT YOU DO

1. Enlarge and trace the tree topper patterns, opposite. Cut out both pieces of pattern and tape together along sides labeled A. Trace pattern onto kraft paper and cut out. Repeat four times.

2. Use a crafts knife and ruler to lightly score along dotted lines. Use bone folder to fold along scored lines. Connect tab B to opposite side marked B using glue stick. Score and fold remaining four pieces of paper; glue tab B to side B on each. Once all five points of star are created, glue them together at tabs labeled C and D. Slip a dowel into bottom or glue a piece of wire at bottom to connect topper to your tree.

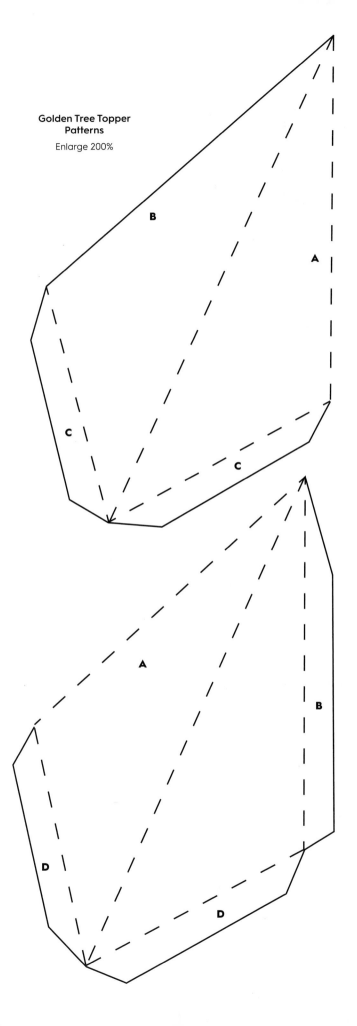

Golden Tree Topper Patterns

Enlarge 200%

TASSEL PACKAGES

Handmade paper tassels add a playful touch to a traditional gift box wrapped in paper decorated with metallic paint pens or gold leaf. Once you've wrapped your gifts, put them on display.

WHAT YOU NEED

Kraft paper, both plain and gold-leaf (see page 93) • Crafts glue • Ribbon • Scissors

WHAT YOU DO

1. Cut ½-inch-wide strips of plain kraft paper into twelve 10-inch lengths. Lay strips in a starburst pattern, gluing each strip to the one on top of it. Let dry.

2. Loosely bend bundle of strips in half to form a tassel. Glue a strip of gold-leaf kraft paper around the bundle 1 inch from top. For a hanger, slip ribbon through the opening below where the strips are folded over.

SET THE SCENE

Add festive flair to your Christmas table by using plenty of gold accents. Use gold leaf and gold paint to dress up everything from pinecones to dinnerware. Throw in plenty of natural elements like a burlap runner and sprigs of greenery to balance the bling with more humble notes.

Simple stemware becomes the center of attention when decorated with oodles of doodles using gold glass paint. Each piece will be wonderfully unique and makes a much-appreciated take-home gift for each holiday guest.

STRIPE IT RICH

Warm up your table settings with touches of gold, opposite. Spray-on fabric paint is an easy and inexpensive way to get a basic white napkin in the holiday spirit. Gather the decorated napkin into a pretty ring and finish the look by tucking in a sprig of greenery.

WHAT YOU NEED

Plain white dinner napkins • Foam crafts sticker • Painters tape • Metallic gold spray fabric paint

WHAT YOU DO

1. On the front of a plain napkin, place a holiday-theme sticker, like a Christmas tree, in the desired spot.

2. Tape off portions of the napkin. Spray the unmasked part of the napkin, including over the sticker, with gold fabric paint. Remove the tape and sticker. Allow the napkin to dry completely before using.

GILDED WINEGLASS

WHAT YOU NEED

Wineglass • Gold glass paint (we used Pēbēo Vitrea 160)

WHAT YOU DO

1. Be sure the glass is clean and dry. Plan the design and then draw tiny doodles onto the base of a wineglass using the pointed nozzle that comes with the paint. Continue adding doodles until the desired effect is achieved.

2. Bake the finished glass, following manufacturer's instructions.

Shining Star

Poinsettia Wrap

happy
holidays

Please Hold

Straws on
Strings

Scalloped Border

Golden Deer

Bottlebrush Bauble

SHINING STAR
Shiny ribbon shaped into a bow gets a touch of personalization.

POINSETTIA WRAP
Raid the faux-floral aisle for dramatic toppers to pair with floral pattern paper.

SCALLOPED BORDER
Offset a simple ribbon embellishment with an unusual border made from washi tape.

GOLDEN DEER
An ornament for a miniature tree gets repurposed as a tag embellishment.

PLEASE HOLD
A household clothespin adds a surprising, yet functional, touch to a regular package.

STRAWS ON STRINGS
Paper straws and glitter washi tape bring a touch of modern glam to an ordinary package.

BOTTLEBRUSH BAUBLE
A vintage-look bottlebrush tree is a glittery finish to a gift wrapped in touches of gold.

ALL WRAPPED UP

Adding gold leaf to basic kraft paper or to pretty textured paper makes for standout gifts under the tree. The results are so beautiful you'll want to use your packages as decorations

WHAT YOU NEED
Kraft or specialty decorative paper • Gold-leaf adhesive • Foam brush • Gold leaf • Small paintbrush or a second foam brush

WHAT YOU DO
1. Cover desired areas of the paper with adhesive by painting it on (for simple strokes) or dipping a paintbrush into the adhesive and flicking the bristles (for splatters).
2. When the adhesive is tacky, carefully lay a sheet of gold leaf over it and gently press in place. Use a paintbrush or clean foam brush to gently brush away excess gold leaf. Let dry completely before wrapping gifts in the paper.

SEQUIN MINI STOCKINGS

Add some shimmer and shine to your tree or package with these glittery stockings all in bright holiday colors.

WHAT YOU NEED

Tracing paper • Pencil • Scissors • Sequin fabric in desired colors • Scissors • Sewing machine • Thread to match colors

WHAT YOU DO

1. Enlarge and trace patterns, below and right. Trace around patterns on sequin fabric; cut out.
2. Fold the front top band and the back top band in half, wrong sides together, and stitch along the bottom (raw edge).
3. Line up sewn edge of the front top band to the top of the front stocking, right sides together, and sew across the top. Repeat with the back top band and back stocking.
4. Put right sides together of front and back stockings and sew around the outside. Turn right side out.

Sequin Mini Stockings Patterns

Enlarge 300%

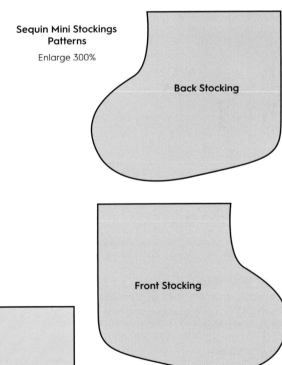

Back Stocking

Front Stocking

Front Top Band

Back Top Band

TINSEL POM-POM

Tinsel garland takes on a new dimension when it is spiraled to form a happy holiday trim.

WHAT YOU NEED

Foam ball ornaments such as Styrofoam • Tinsel garland in desired color • Hot-glue gun and glue sticks • Narrow gold ribbon for hanging

WHAT YOU DO

1. Starting at the top of the foam ball ornament, attach tinsel garland to the ball by wrapping it around and gluing in small areas at a time until you reach the bottom of the ornament.
2. Add a ribbon for hanging.

FESTIVE POM-POM WREATH

Little pom-poms in all sizes and colors combine to make a fanciful wreath to carry you into the new year.

WHAT YOU NEED

Foam wreath form such as Styrofoam in desired size • Pom-poms in desired sizes and colors • Hot-glue gun and glue sticks • Narrow ribbon for hanging

WHAT YOU DO

1. Starting on one side of the wreath, glue pom-poms to the wreath, working on small areas at a time. Continue until entire wreath is covered.
2. Add a loop of ribbon for hanging.

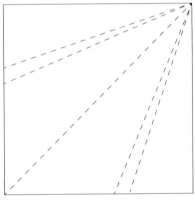

**Glitter Paper Wreath
Template**

Enlarge 300%

GOLD DOILY TREE

WHAT YOU NEED

Aluminum foil • Plastic foam tree form such as Styrofoam •
Lace doilies • Decoupage medium such as Mod Podge •
Sewing pins • Gold paint (craft or spray) • Glitter, optional •
Narrow gold ribbon • Small purchased stars • Hot-glue gun
and glue sticks

WHAT YOU DO

1. Wrap tree form with aluminum foil. **Note:** This will help keep
the doilies from sticking.
2. Position doilies around the tree form, securing with sewing
pins. When you have the desired look, apply a thick layer
of decoupage medium onto the doily. When dry, apply
another coat.
3. Let dry; remove the doilies from the tree form gently.
TIP: Use a butter knife to separate the inside of the doily
tree from the outside of the tree form. Remove any pieces
of aluminum foil from the tree. Paint with one more coat of
decoupage medium; let dry.
4. Paint doily tree with crafts paint or spray paint; let dry.
Apply a thin coat of decoupage medium around tree and dust
with glitter.
5. Tie the ribbon in a bow and hot-glue the bow and some
stars at the top of the tree.

GLITTER PAPER WREATH

*Almost like magic, flat sheets of glittery cardstock are
folded into a stunning holiday wreath for your door.*

WHAT YOU NEED

Tracing paper • Pencil • Scissors • 12×12-inch glitter
cardstock in desired metallic shades • Crafts knife such as
X-acto • Ruler • Glitter paper wreath template • Hot-glue
gun and glue sticks • Flat wreath form • Narrow red ribbon

WHAT YOU DO

1. Enlarge and trace template on tracing paper. Cut glitter
cardstock sheets into quarters (6×6-inch square pieces). You'll
need ten 6-inch squares.
2. To create each section, on the outside of the cardstock,
score each piece of paper where indicated on the template
illustration, above.
3. Fold outside corners together and secure with hot glue.
When all 10 sections are done, attach them to a wreath form
using hot glue.
4. Add a ribbon for hanging.

Playful Paper

Decorate all through the house with charming Christmas trims fashioned from pretty papers and festive embellishments.

PLAYFUL PAPER FOREST

Simple paper circles in shades of green transform into 3-D trees with tiny birch trunks.

WHAT YOU NEED

Tracing paper • Pencil • Scissors • 12×12-inch sheet of green cardstock (1 sheet per tree) • Paper tube from paper towel roll • Hot-glue gun and glue sticks • Crafts knife such as X-acto and cutting board • Ruler • Thick twig for base • Purchased star shape for topper

WHAT YOU DO

1. Cut three circles, each 6×6 inches in diameter, from cardstock. **Note:** If you are making more than one tree, choose different shades of green and mix and match the green colors for each tree.

2. Enlarge and trace templates, below. Referring to the templates, score the circle in eighths. Turn paper over and score the circle in eighths again, in alternate spaces. See template illustration, below. Fold paper on score lines on both sides of paper to form zigzag shape.

3. Cut a 1-inch strip off the paper tube. Using hot glue, attach it to the inside of the tree form to secure the shape. Repeat process three times to form all three layers of the tree. Secure layers on top using hot glue.

4. Cut the twig to fit as a trunk. Hot-glue in place. Hot-glue the star at the top of the tree.

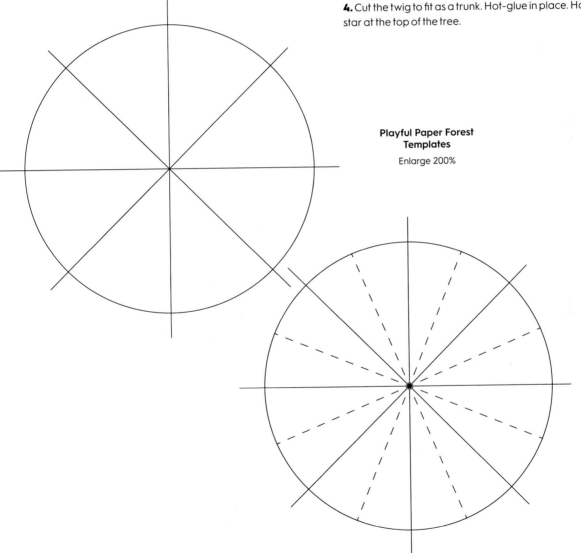

Playful Paper Forest Templates

Enlarge 200%

NEUTRAL NEWSPAPER TREE

Soft petals made of newspaper bunch together for an earthy yet delicate tree.

WHAT YOU NEED

Flower punch (see Sources, page 160) or use template provided • Scissors • Newspaper • Foam tree form such as Styrofoam • Straight pins • Thumbtacks

WHAT YOU DO

1. Cut petals out of newspaper using flower punch. Or, to use template, trace the template, right. Cut out and trace onto newspaper. Cut out shapes using scissors.

2. Starting at the bottom of the tree, attach petals to tree form using thumbtacks and/or straight pins. Continue adding the shapes until the entire tree is covered.

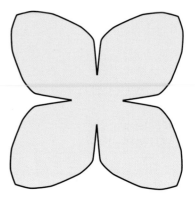

**Neutral Newspaper Tree
Pattern**

Full-Size Pattern

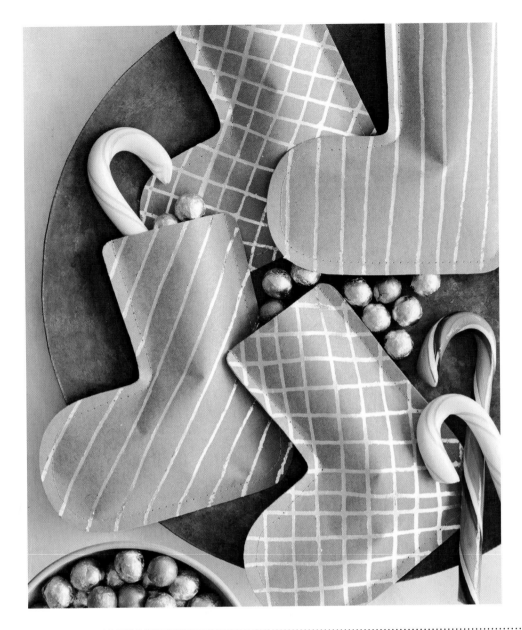

Brown kraft paper is cut into festive stocking shapes, decorated with simple gold lines, and then stitched together to hold all kinds of Christmas goodies.

STOCKING GIFT BAGS

Simple stocking gift bags are a fun alternative to gift wrap and can be made in the blink of an eye.

WHAT YOU NEED
Tracing paper • Pencil • Scissors • Kraft paper • Metallic gold marker • Sewing machine

WHAT YOU DO
1. Enlarge and trace template, right. Using the template as a guide, cut a pair of stocking shapes from kraft paper. Use a gold metallic paint pen or marker to make lines or a grid on the paper.

2. Use a sewing machine to stitch around the edge of the stocking shape, keeping the top open.

Stocking Gift Bags Pattern

Enlarge 300%

Count down to Christmas with a festive and fun paper calendar to mark each of the 12 days. Each little pocket holds a special idea to do together.

12-DAYS PAPER COUNTDOWN

Plan an activity for each of the 12 days of Christmas, and make a playful paper calendar to keep track of the special days.

WHAT YOU NEED

Acrylic paint • 18×14-inch bulletin board • Patterned paper • Crafts glue (optional) • Double-sided tape • Twelve 2¼×3½-inch red coin envelopes • Number stamps 0—9 • Black ink pad • 1¼-inch diameter white sticker labels • Hot-glue gun and glue sticks • 1¼-inch-diameter metal tag trims • White paper slips

WHAT YOU DO

1. Paint the frame of the bulletin board and let dry. Apply patterned paper to the face of the board with crafts glue or double-sided tape.
2. Cut off the flaps of each red coin envelope to leave an open top. Space the envelopes evenly on the bulletin board and attach with double-sided tape.
3. Stamp numbers 1—12 onto sticker labels and attach to envelopes. Apply hot glue to metal tag trims and attach to round stickers.
4. Write or print activities for each of the 12 days on white paper slips. Insert slips into envelopes.

QUILLED FRILLS

Shape narrow strips of paper into coils, curves, and loops to make this fanciful quilled ornament. Establish the round outline by wrapping a paper strip around a jar, then add segments and curly details to fill in the elegant ornament.

WHAT YOU NEED

⅛-inch-wide quilling paper: bright pink, pale pink, white, silver, black • 2-inch-diameter jar or bottle • Crafts glue • Needle-nose applicator or toothpick (to apply glue) • 6-inch square of waxed paper • 6-inch square of corkboard or cardboard • Straight pins • Quilling tool (needle tool or slotted tool) or toothpick • 8-inch length of ⅛-inch-wide ribbon or bakers twine

WHAT YOU DO

FORM THE ORNAMENT CONTOUR

1. Cut a 30-inch strip from bright pink quilling paper. Wrap the strip tightly around a 2-inch-diameter jar, applying a very thin line of glue as you go to secure each layer of paper. Keep the paper layers directly on top of each other as you wrap and glue; let dry.

2. Place the waxed paper square on top of the corkboard or cardboard square and pin each corner to secure.

Note: This will be the work board where you build the rest of the ornament.

3. Gently push the bright pink paper circle off the end of the jar. Pin the circle to the work board.

FORM THE OUTER AND INNER SEGMENTS

1. Cut an 8-inch strip from both bright pink and pale pink quilling paper. Glue the strips back-to-back using a very thin line of glue on the entire length; let dry.

2. Cut a 6-inch strip from both pale pink and white. Glue the strips back-to-back; let dry.

3. Cut the bright pink/pale pink strip in half and run a thumbnail along each half to slightly curve it. To make one outer segment, line up one end of one strip at the inner top center of ornament, with the curve toward the outer edge and the other end at the bottom center of ornament, making sure the bright pink side faces out. Cut off any excess. Glue ends to ornament and pin until dry. Repeat on opposite side of the ornament to create the other outer segment.

4. Cut the pale pink/white strip in half. Use thumbnail to make a very slight curve in each half. Line up one end of one strip at the inner top center of ornament inside the outer segments, with the curve toward the outer edge and the other end at the center bottom, making sure the pale pink side faces out. Cut off any excess. Glue ends and pin until dry. Repeat on the opposite side of the ornament to create the other inner segment.

ADD THE LOOPS AND COILS

1. Cut twelve 1-inch strips from bright pink. Create a loop from one 1-inch strip. Referring to photo, above right, and using a very small dot of glue on each end, secure loop at bottom of one outside segment. Loop a second 1-inch strip and tuck

ends on either side of the first loop, securing with small dots of glue. Repeat, adding a third 1-inch loop on top of the second loop. Repeat, adding three 1-inch loops in remaining bottom and tops of outside segments.

2. Cut twelve 1-inch strips from pale pink. Repeat in the same manner, making and securing loops inside the inner segments.

3. Cut two 10-inch strips from white. Using the quilling tool, coil each strip, glue ends, and pinch into a teardrop. Glue one teardrop into the bottom of the center segment. Cut four 2-inch strips from white. Form one strip into a loop; glue and tuck ends around teardrop. Repeat, adding a second loop over the first loop. Repeat, adding remaining teardrop and two loops at top of center segment.

ADD THE CAP AND HANGER

1. Cut a 2-inch strip of silver; shape strip into a rectangular cap. Glue cap on top of ornament; glue and pin until dry. Using quilling tool, roll a 3-inch silver strip into a loose S shape. Glue the S shape inside cap; let dry.

2. Using quilling tool, coil a 6-inch black strip. Stretch out coil, then reshape with fingers to create an open circle with a small coil inside. Glue end of strip, then glue coil to top of cap; let dry.

3. Add narrow ribbon or bakers twine to top of ornament as a hanging loop.

POTATO-PRINT TREE WRAP

A humble potato becomes a favorite stamping tool to make quick-to-print wrapping paper.

WHAT YOU NEED

Tracing paper • Pencil • Scissors • Potato • Knife • Pencil • Paper towels • Small piece of paper or paper plate • Acrylic paint • Kraft paper on a roll

WHAT YOU DO

1. Be sure the potato is clean and dry. Cut the potato in half.
2. Referring to the template, right, draw the tree shape or other desired shape to the outside edge of the potato. Cut out the area around the design.
3. Pat the potato with paper towels to remove any moisture. Place a small amount of paint onto a piece of paper or plate. Press the potato into the paint and repeatedly stamp the paper to make designs on the kraft paper, dipping into the paint as needed.

Potato-Print Tree Wrap Pattern

Full-Size Pattern

WINTER WONDERLAND CARD

Share a white Christmas by creating this stunning Christmas card made from white cardstock with little circles of light.

WHAT YOU NEED

Tracing paper • Pencil • Scissors • 12×12 inch piece of white cardstock • Small hole punch • Foam adhesive squares • A6 size blank greeting card

WHAT YOU DO

1. Enlarge and trace template and trace onto cardstock. Cut pieces (front layer, middle layer, and back layer) using template as a guide.

2. Use small hole punch to punch out circles at top of the back layer of the card pieces.

3. Attach each layer together and onto the card with foam adhesive squares.

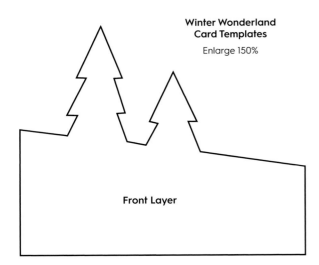

Winter Wonderland Card Templates

Enlarge 150%

Front Layer

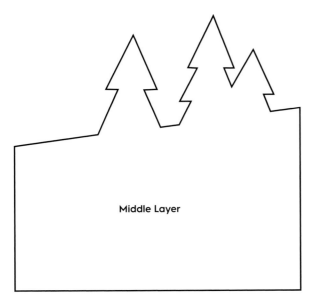

Middle Layer

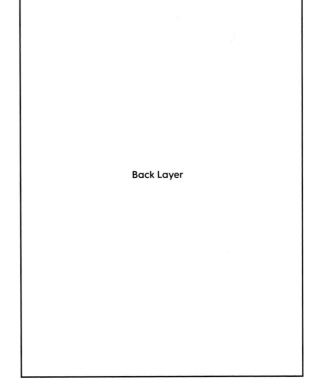

Back Layer

PAPER STRAW PACKAGES

Create simple package toppers by using muffin liners, washi tape, and paper straws. No matter what size box you are embellishing, bits of paper can add a pop of color and style. Flatten cupcake liners for flower tops and cut colorful paper straws and make flower stems. Piece together a little tree from straws and add washi tape trims.

SPECIAL DELIVERY

Use simple paper shapes and paper stickers to make quick work of package wrapping. Dangle mittens from striped cotton twine and a bow. Scallop the edges of a purchased tag with a ¼-inch paper punch to mimic a vintage postage stamp. To give the appearance of a mailed package with a striped tag, place a postage stamp in the top right corner and stamp over it with a postmark-theme rubber stamp.

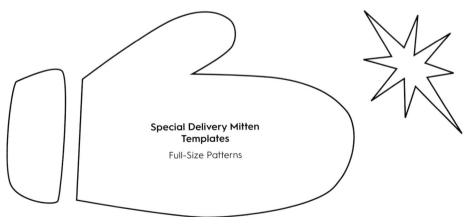

Special Delivery Mitten Templates

Full-Size Patterns

PHOTO-FINISH WRAPS

Custom gift wrappings don't get any more personal than these packages. Double-sided wrapping paper flips back to reveal photos that serve either as visual name tags for the gift recipients or as a way to relive special moments with loved ones. For an added touch, use a marker to write a sweet sentiment on the photo.

WHAT YOU NEED

Double-sided wrapping paper • Double-stick tape • Ruler • Pencil • Black-and-white photo (or photocopy of a photo) • Crafts knife • Cotton twine • 2 two-hole buttons • Ribbon

WHAT YOU DO

1. Wrap the box, taping to secure loose edges. Using a ruler and pencil, draw a square or rectangle on the front of the wrapped box slightly smaller than the photo. Using the crafts knife, gently cut along the top and bottom of the square or rectangle and then down the center. Be sure that you don't cut through the box top.

2. Turn cut center edges outward and tape them to the package to create shutter-like flaps that show the reverse side of the wrapping paper. Thread a piece of twine through holes in each button. Tape a threaded button on each flap. Adhere tape to the back of the photo. Slip the photo into the opening, taping to the top of the box to secure.

3. Tie a piece of ribbon into a bow. Tape to the package above the photo opening.

SPREAD-THE-WORD WRAPS

Stencil-inspired letter cutouts and washi tape perk up
white cardstock bands wrapped around solid paper.
Finish the packages with purchased coordinating tags.

WHAT YOU NEED

Alphabet stencils • White computer paper • White
cardstock • Crafts knife • Cutting mat • Box (small enough
to wrap cardstock around) • Solid-color red and lime green
wrapping paper • Double-stick tape • Ribbon
• Washi tape • Cotton twine • ¼-inch paper punch • Gift tag
• ¼-inch white paper hole reinforcement circle, (optional)

WHAT YOU DO

1. Use the stencils to make patterns for the words **PEACE** and
NOEL on white paper to fit your box.

2. Place the word pattern on a piece of cardstock, about
2 inches from the bottom. Test to make sure it will be centered
on the front of the box. Tape the corners of the pattern to the
cardstock. Working on the cutting mat, use the crafts knife
to cut out each letter. Embellish the long edges of the cutout
cardstock with washi tape.

3. Wrap the box with wrapping paper. Wrap the embellished
cardstock around the box, centering the cutout word on front
and taping in back with washi tape.

4. Wrap ribbon around the box, placing it toward the top of
the cardstock band and tying it into a bow on the front center.
Punch a hole in the top center of the tag. If desired, place a
reinforcement circle around the punched hole. Thread twine
through the hole. Tie the tag to the ribbon.

The One-Pan Plan

Got friends or family coming to visit for a few days? Employ a simple strategy for feeding hungry houseguests delicious food with the least amount of effort: the one-pan/one-pot/one-dish recipe. Whether it's a bubbly casserole, gooey sandwich, or slow cooker stew, these tasty dishes will keep things merry and bright.

RAVIOLI LASAGNA WITH BABY KALE AND ITALIAN SAUSAGE

Celebrate Christmas with this red, white, and green dish. Kale not only adds a bright green color, but it's also packed full of vitamins.

WHAT YOU NEED

1   5- to 6-oz. pkg. baby kale, coarsely chopped
12 oz. Italian-flavor cooked chicken sausage, chopped
1½ cups shredded mozzarella cheese (6 oz.)
½   cup snipped fresh basil
1   28-oz. can no-salt-added crushed tomatoes
1   14.5-oz. can fire-roasted diced tomatoes with garlic, undrained
1   8-oz. can no-salt-added tomato sauce
1   tsp. dried Italian seasoning, crushed
½   tsp. fennel seeds, crushed
2   9-oz. pkg. refrigerated cheese-filled ravioli
    Grated Parmesan cheese (optional)

WHAT YOU DO

1. Preheat oven to 375°F. Grease a 3-qt. rectangular baking dish. In a large bowl combine kale, sausage, ¾ cup of the mozzarella cheese, and the basil. For sauce, in another large bowl combine the next five ingredients (through fennel seeds).
2. Spread about 1 cup of the sauce in prepared dish. Top with half of the ravioli and kale mixture. Spoon another 1 cup

of the sauce over kale mixture. Top with remaining ravioli, kale mixture, and sauce. Sprinkle with remaining ¾ cup mozzarella cheese.
3. Cover with nonstick or greased foil. Bake 30 minutes. Remove foil; bake 25 minutes more or until heated through. If desired, top with Parmesan cheese and additional basil. Makes 8 servings.

UPSIDE-DOWN PIZZA CASSEROLE

Here's a deep-dish pizza that's fast and easy to make. Use premade refrigerated pizza dough and tomato sauce with the seasonings already added to save on prep time.

WHAT YOU NEED

1½ lb. lean ground beef or bulk Italian sausage
1½ cups sliced fresh mushrooms (4 oz.)
1   15-oz. can tomato sauce with Italian seasonings
¼   cup sliced pitted ripe olives (optional)
1   to 1½ cups shredded mozzarella cheese or Italian-blend cheeses (4 to 6 oz.)
1   13.8-oz. pkg. refrigerated pizza dough
    Toppers: Milk, Parmesan, crushed red pepper (optional)

WHAT YOU DO

1. Preheat oven to 400°F. In a large skillet cook ground beef and mushrooms over medium-high heat until meat is browned, using a wooden spoon to break up meat as it cooks.

Drain off fat. Stir in tomato sauce and, if desired, olives; heat through. Transfer meat mixture to a 2-qt. rectangular baking dish. Sprinkle with cheese.

2. Top mixture in baking dish with pizza dough, either whole or cut into rectangular pieces, sealing dough to edges of baking dish. If desired, brush with milk and sprinkle with shredded Parmesan. Bake, uncovered, 20 to 25 minutes or until dough is golden brown. Let stand 5 minutes before serving. If desired, sprinkle with red pepper flakes. Makes 6 servings.

CHEESEBURGER SHEPHERD'S PIE

Kids and adults alike will love this family-style casserole. It has all of the great flavors of a cheeseburger baked together in one dish.

WHAT YOU NEED

1½ lb. russet potatoes, peeled and cut up
½ cup light sour cream
¼ cup milk
½ tsp. salt
1 cup shredded cheddar cheese (4 oz.)
1½ lb. lean ground beef
¾ cup chopped red and/or green sweet pepper
½ cup chopped onion
2 cloves garlic, minced

1½ cups frozen whole kernel corn
1 cup water
1 6-oz. can tomato paste
½ cup coarsely chopped dill pickles
¼ cup yellow mustard
1 tsp. dried oregano, crushed
  Sliced green onions and/or crisp-cooked bacon (optional)

WHAT YOU DO

1. Preheat oven to 350°F. In a covered large saucepan cook potatoes in enough boiling lightly salted water to cover 15 to 20 minutes or until tender; drain. Mash potatoes. Gradually beat in sour cream, milk, and salt. Stir in ½ cup of the cheese.

2. Meanwhile, in a large skillet cook the next four ingredients (through garlic) over medium-high heat until meat is browned. Drain off fat. Stir in the next six ingredients (through oregano). Bring to boiling; reduce heat. Simmer, uncovered, 5 minutes to blend flavors. Stir in remaining ½ cup cheese.

3. Transfer meat mixture to a 2½-qt. shallow baking dish. Spoon mashed potatoes in mounds onto meat mixture. Sprinkle with additional cheese. Bake 20 minutes or until heated through and cheese is melted. If desired, top with green onions and/or bacon. Makes 6 servings.

13×9 HOT SANDWICH MELTS

Need sandwiches for a crowd? Simply assemble all of the sandwiches in one dish and bake. Serve with chips or fresh-cut veggies and your meal is complete.

WHAT YOU NEED
12 Rolls, split
    Filling
    Drizzle

WHAT YOU DO
1. Preheat oven to 350°F. Arrange bottoms of Rolls in a 13×9-inch baking pan or 3-qt. rectangular baking dish. Add Filling and tops of Rolls. Spoon Drizzle over sandwiches.
2. Cover pan with foil. Bake 15 minutes. Remove foil; bake 10 to 15 minutes more or until cheese is melted and roll tops are light brown. Makes 12 servings.

Veggie Reuben Pretzel Melts Line baking pan with foil and coat foil with nonstick cooking spray. **Rolls:** Use 3-inch pretzel rolls. **Filling:** Layer roll bottoms with 2 cups fresh spinach leaves; 1 cup thinly sliced roasted red sweet peppers, well drained; and ½ cup each thinly sliced red onion and cucumber. Spoon 1 cup sauerkraut, well drained, onto vegetables. Top with 6 oz. thinly sliced Swiss cheese. Spread cut sides of roll tops with ½ cup Thousand Island salad dressing. **Drizzle:** Combine 6 Tbsp. melted butter, 1 Tbsp. coarse ground mustard, 1 tsp. crushed caraway seeds, and ½ tsp. minced dried onion. Bake, covered, 30 minutes.

Italian Roast Beef Sourdough Melts **Rolls:** Use 3-inch sourdough rolls. **Filling:** Layer roll bottoms with 12 oz. thinly sliced deli-style roast beef and 1½ cups chopped pickled mixed vegetables (giardiniera). Top with 6 oz. thinly sliced provolone or mozzarella cheese. Spread cut sides of roll tops with one 8-oz. tub cream cheese spread with garden vegetables. **Drizzle:** Combine ¼ cup olive oil; 2 cloves minced garlic; 1 tsp. dried Italian seasoning, crushed; and ½ tsp. crushed red pepper. Bake, covered, 30 minutes.

SMOKY CHICKEN AND CHEESY POTATO CASSEROLE

This hearty potato-and-meat casserole will warm up a crowd on a cold winter day. Use frozen hash brown potatoes with onion and sweet peppers for added flavor and color.

WHAT YOU NEED

1   10.75-oz. can condensed cream of chicken with herbs soup
1   8-oz. carton sour cream
1½   cups shredded smoked cheddar cheese (6 oz.)
1   28-oz. pkg. frozen diced hash brown potatoes with onions and peppers, thawed
1   lb. smoked or roasted chicken or turkey, cut into bite-size strips
1   cup crushed croutons (optional)
1   Tbsp. butter, melted (optional)
     Fresh thyme (optional)

WHAT YOU DO

1. Preheat oven to 350°F. Lightly grease a 3-qt. rectangular baking dish; set aside. In a large bowl combine soup, sour cream, and cheese. Stir in potatoes and chicken. Transfer chicken mixture to the prepared baking dish.
2. If desired, in a small bowl combine crushed croutons and melted butter; sprinkle over potato mixture.
3. Bake, uncovered, 40 to 50 minutes or until heated through. If desired, garnish with fresh thyme. Makes 12 servings.

ROASTED SAUSAGE WITH MUSHROOMS, SQUASH, AND POLENTA

Either plain or Italian-flavor polenta works well in this dish. Look for precooked, ready-to-serve polenta in the refrigerated section of the store. Or check out the aisle with dried pastas for a shelf-stable version.

WHAT YOU NEED

1   16-oz. tube refrigerated cooked polenta, cut into ½-inch slices and halved
2   cups sliced fresh cremini mushrooms
2   cups cubed, peeled butternut squash
3   Tbsp. olive oil
     Salt and black pepper
1   lb. uncooked mild Italian sausage links
1   tsp. snipped fresh rosemary

WHAT YOU DO

1. Preheat oven to 425°F. In a 15×10-inch baking pan combine polenta, mushrooms, and squash. Drizzle with oil and sprinkle with salt and pepper.
2. Prick each sausage a few times with a fork. Place in pan with vegetables. Sprinkle with rosemary.
3. Roast 30 minutes or until sausages are done (160°F), stirring once. If desired, top with additional rosemary. Makes 6 servings.

CHICKEN SOUP WITH CHIVE DUMPLINGS

Homemade soup doesn't require an entire day in the kitchen. This takes slightly less than an hour to make. And, if you're really short on time, simply make the soup ahead and prepare the dumplings just before serving.

WHAT YOU NEED

1   lb. skinless, boneless chicken breast halves
    Salt and black pepper
2   Tbsp. olive oil
1   cup chopped carrots (2 medium)
1   cup chopped celery (2 stalks)
⅓   cup chopped leek (1 medium)
6   cups chicken broth
4   sprigs fresh thyme
1   bay leaf
1½ cups all-purpose flour
1   Tbsp. snipped fresh chives
2   tsp. baking powder
1   tsp. salt
3   Tbsp. cold butter
¾   cup milk
¼   cup snipped fresh Italian parsley

WHAT YOU DO

1. Sprinkle chicken with salt and pepper. In a 4- to 5-qt. Dutch oven heat oil over medium-high heat. Cook chicken in hot oil until brown on both sides. Reduce heat to medium. Cook, covered, 7 to 9 minutes more or until chicken is no longer pink (170°F). Remove chicken from pan.

2. Add carrots, celery, and leek to Dutch oven. Cook, covered, 5 to 7 minutes or until vegetables are tender, stirring occasionally.

3. Cut chicken into ½-inch pieces. Return chicken to Dutch oven. Add broth, thyme, and bay leaf. Bring to boiling; reduce heat. Simmer, uncovered, 15 minutes.

4. Meanwhile, for dumplings, in a medium bowl stir together flour, chives, baking powder, and the 1 tsp. salt. Using a pastry blender, cut in butter until mixture resembles coarse crumbs. Stir in milk just until combined.

5. Remove and discard thyme sprigs and bay leaf. Stir in parsley; season to taste with additional salt and pepper. Bring to boiling. Drop dumpling dough by large spoonfuls onto hot bubbling soup. Cook, uncovered, 10 minutes. Reduce heat to medium-low. Cook, covered, about 10 minutes more or until a wooden toothpick inserted in the centers of dumplings comes out clean. Makes 6 servings.

Vegetable Soup with Chive Dumplings Prepare as directed, except substitute vegetable broth for the chicken broth and omit the chicken.

To Make Ahead Prepare as directed through Step 3. Cover and chill up to 3 days. To serve, bring soup to boiling. Continue as directed in Step 4.

PORK, PORTOBELLO, AND MASHED ROOTS SHEPHERD'S PIE

Portobello mushrooms add a warm, earthy flavor to this dish. If portobello mushrooms are unavailable, use cremini mushrooms, also called "baby bella" or "baby portobello."

WHAT YOU NEED
1½ lb. lean ground pork
6   cups stemmed and chopped fresh portobello mushrooms (16 oz.)
1   cup chopped onion (1 large)
6   cloves garlic, minced
1¼ cups reduced-sodium chicken broth
1   cup sliced celery (2 stalks)
1   cup chopped carrots (2 medium)
3   Tbsp. quick-cooking tapioca
2   Tbsp. Worcestershire sauce
1   tsp. dried thyme, crushed
½   tsp. salt
¼   tsp. black pepper
2   cups peeled and chopped rutabaga
1   cup peeled and chopped potato (1 medium)
1   cup peeled and chopped parsnips (2 medium)
1   cup chopped carrots (2 medium)
¼   cup low-fat milk
½   tsp. salt
1   cup frozen peas
     Snipped fresh chives

WHAT YOU DO
1. In a 4- to 5-qt. Dutch oven cook ground pork, mushrooms, onion, and garlic over medium-high heat until meat is browned and mushrooms are tender, using a wooden spoon to break up meat as it cooks. Drain off fat.

2. In a 4-qt. slow cooker combine meat mixture with the next eight ingredients (through pepper). Cover and cook on low-heat setting 7 to 8 hours or on high 3½ to 4 hours.

3. About 1 hour before serving, in a covered large saucepan cook rutabaga, potato, parsnips, and 1 cup carrots in enough boiling water to cover 25 to 30 minutes or until vegetables are very tender; drain. Return vegetables to hot pan. Mash vegetables with a potato masher. Stir in milk and ½ tsp. salt.

4. If using low-heat setting, turn cooker to high. Stir frozen peas into mixture in cooker; spoon the mashed vegetables evenly over mixture. Cover and cook 30 minutes more. Before serving, sprinkle with chives. Makes 6 servings.

BEEF STEW POT PIE

Cubed croissants create a light, flaky top crust on this beef-and-vegetable pot pie.

WHAT YOU NEED
     Nonstick cooking spray
¼   cup butter
3   croissants, split
1½ cups coarsely chopped carrots (3 medium)
1½ cups coarsely chopped celery (3 stalks)
1   cup frozen small whole onions, thawed and halved
3   cups sliced fresh mushrooms (8 oz.)
1   cup Burgundy
1   Tbsp. stone-ground Dijon-style mustard
4   cloves garlic, minced
2   tsp. finely snipped fresh rosemary
2   tsp. dried thyme, crushed
½   tsp. freshly ground black pepper
2   17-oz. pkg. refrigerated cooked beef tips with gravy
1   cup 50%-less-sodium beef broth

WHAT YOU DO
1. Preheat oven to 375°F. Coat a 3-qt. rectangular baking dish with cooking spray; set aside.

2. In a small microwave-safe bowl microwave 1 Tbsp. of the butter on 70% power (medium-high) about 30 seconds or until melted. Brush cut sides of croissants with melted butter. Cube croissants; set aside.

3. In a large skillet heat the remaining 3 Tbsp. butter over medium heat until melted. Add carrots, celery, and onions. Cook 7 to 9 minutes or just until vegetables are tender, stirring occasionally. Carefully stir in mushrooms, Burgundy, mustard, garlic, rosemary, thyme, and pepper. Bring to boiling; reduce heat. Simmer, uncovered, 5 minutes. Stir in beef with gravy and the broth; heat through.

4. Transfer hot meat mixture to the prepared baking dish. Sprinkle with cubed croissants. Bake, uncovered, 20 to 25 minutes or until meat mixture is bubbly and croissants are golden. Makes 8 servings.

APPLE AND CHEDDAR PENNE PIE

Panko bread crumbs tossed with a little butter make a crispy crust for this mac 'n' cheese pie.

WHAT YOU NEED

2	Tbsp. butter, softened
⅔	cup panko bread crumbs
1	Tbsp. snipped fresh thyme
12	oz. dried penne pasta (3½ cups)
3	Tbsp. butter
2	cups peeled and chopped tart cooking apples (3 medium)
½	cup chopped sweet onion, such as Vidalia or Walla Walla (1 medium)
3	Tbsp. all-purpose flour
½	tsp. salt
¼	tsp. black pepper
2	cups whole milk
½	cup apple cider
2	3-oz. pkg. cream cheese, softened and cut up
1½	cups shredded white cheddar cheese (6 oz.)
	Very thinly sliced, unpeeled tart cooking apple (optional)
	Fresh thyme sprigs (optional)

WHAT YOU DO

1. Preheat oven to 350°F. Grease the bottom and sides of a 10-inch springform pan with 1 Tbsp. of the softened butter. Sprinkle sides of pan with ⅓ cup of the panko to coat; set aside. Melt the remaining 1 Tbsp. softened butter. Stir in the remaining ⅓ cup panko and 1 tsp. of the snipped thyme; set aside.

2. Cook pasta according to package directions, except cook 2 minutes less than the suggested time; drain. Return pasta to pan.

3. Meanwhile, in a large saucepan heat the 3 Tbsp. butter over medium heat until melted. Add the chopped apples and onion; cook 5 to 8 minutes or until tender, stirring frequently. Stir in flour, salt, and pepper; cook and stir 2 minutes. Gradually stir in milk and apple cider. Cook and stir until thickened and bubbly. Reduce heat to low. Add cream cheese, white cheddar cheese, and the remaining 2 tsp. snipped thyme; cook and stir until cheeses are melted.

4. Add cheese mixture to cooked pasta; stir to combine. Transfer pasta mixture to the prepared springform pan. Sprinkle with the reserved panko mixture.

5. Bake about 40 minutes or until edges are bubbly. If desired, arrange the sliced apple on top of pie. Bake about 2 minutes more or just until apple is tender.

6. Cool in pan on a wire rack 20 minutes. Using a small sharp knife, loosen pie from sides of pan; remove sides of pan. If desired, garnish pie with thyme sprigs. Makes 8 servings.

QUICK LASAGNA CASSEROLE

Choose your pasta style for this lasagna-style dish. Campanelle are bell-shape noodles with ruffled edges and cellantani are fun, corkscrew-shape pasta. Both have ridges for holding and trapping lots of sauce.

WHAT YOU NEED

12	oz. dried campanelle or cellantani pasta
1	lb. bulk Italian sausage
1	large onion, cut into thin wedges
1	cup bite-size strips yellow sweet pepper
3	cloves garlic, minced
1	28-oz. jar marinara sauce
1	tsp. fennel seeds, crushed
1	egg, lightly beaten
1	15-oz. carton ricotta cheese
2	cups shredded Italian-blend cheeses (8 oz.)
	Snipped fresh basil (optional)

WHAT YOU DO

1. Cook pasta according to package directions; drain. Meanwhile, in a large skillet cook sausage, onion, sweet pepper, and garlic over medium-high heat until meat is browned. Drain off fat. Transfer to an extra-large bowl. Stir in marinara sauce, fennel seeds, and cooked pasta. Transfer to a 3-qt. rectangular baking dish.

2. In a medium bowl combine egg, ricotta cheese, and 1 cup of the shredded cheese. Spoon in large mounds onto pasta mixture. Sprinkle with remaining 1 cup shredded cheese. Cover with plastic wrap and chill 2 to 24 hours.

3. Preheat oven to 350°F. Bake, uncovered, 50 to 60 minutes or until heated through. Let stand 10 minutes before serving. If desired, sprinkle with basil. Makes 8 servings.

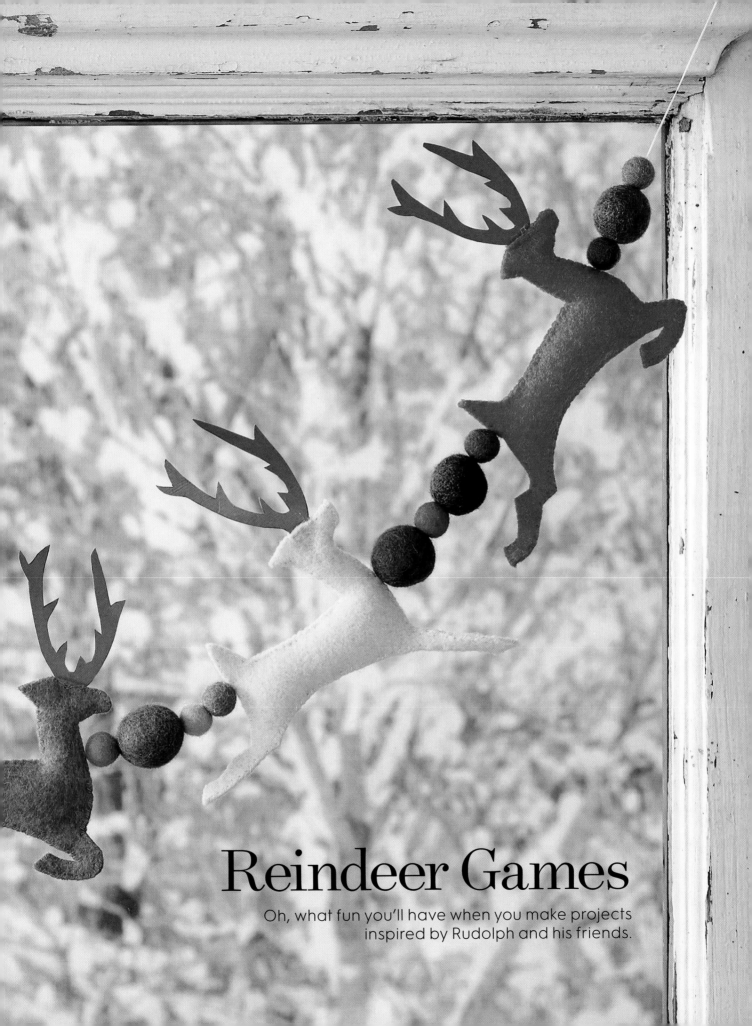

Reindeer Games

Oh, what fun you'll have when you make projects inspired by Rudolph and his friends.

OH, DEER CARDBOARD CUTOUTS

Prancer and Dancer and the gang are fashioned from cardboard to add some life to your holiday table.

WHAT YOU NEED

Tracing paper • Pencil • Scissors • Cardboard box • Crafts knife such as X-acto and cutting mat • Hot-glue gun and glue sticks • Mini pom-pom • Thin marker (optional)

WHAT YOU DO

1. Trace the template patterns, below. Using the templates as a guide, cut shapes out of cardboard using a crafts knife.
2. Attach legs and antlers to body. Use small dots of glue as desired to secure in place.
3. Attach a small pom-pom to the tip of the nose with hot glue. Add a name to the reindeer if using as a place card.

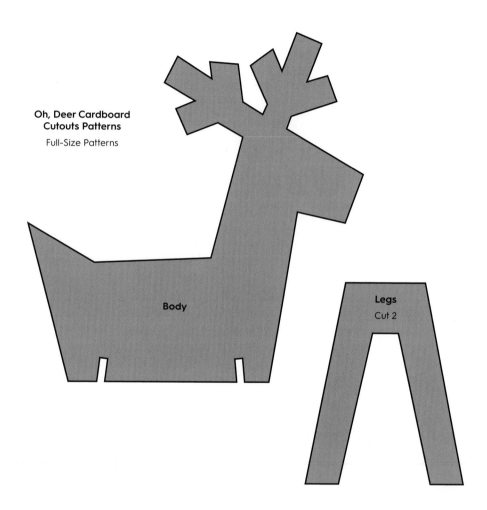

Oh, Deer Cardboard Cutouts Patterns

Full-Size Patterns

Body

Legs
Cut 2

Flat pieces of cardboard come to life when they are cut into little reindeer shapes and slid together to form adorable Christmas creatures. Add a little red or white pom-pom nose for a finishing touch.

FLYING REINDEER GARLAND

Happy colors of nonwoven felt are stitched into little reindeers to fly through the sky on your door or mantel.

WHAT YOU NEED

Tracing paper • Pencil • Nonwoven felt such as National Nonwovens in desired colors (see Sources, page 160) • Scissors • Thread to match fabric colors • Brown cardstock • Hot-glue gun and glue sticks • Bamboo stick (optional) • Purchased felt balls in coordinating colors (see Sources, page 160) • Polyester fiberfill • Fine thread or pearl cotton for stringing deer • Needle

WHAT YOU DO

1. Trace the patterns, opposite, and cut out. Cut out desired number of reindeer from each pattern from desired color of felt.

2. Cut out a pair of antlers from the brown cardstock for each deer. Set aside.

3. Lay the front and back pieces with wrong sides together. Slide the paper antlers in place and use a tiny dot of hot glue to secure.

4. Whip-stitch around the outside of the reindeer shape, leaving about 1 inch open on the underside of the reindeer. Stuff the piece slightly with fiberfill, using a bamboo pick if needed to get into the small areas. Stitch the opening closed.

5. To make the garland, line up the deer in the order desired with felt balls between. Thread the felt balls on the fine thread and attach at the front and back of each reindeer. Tie at the ends to prevent the balls from sliding off.

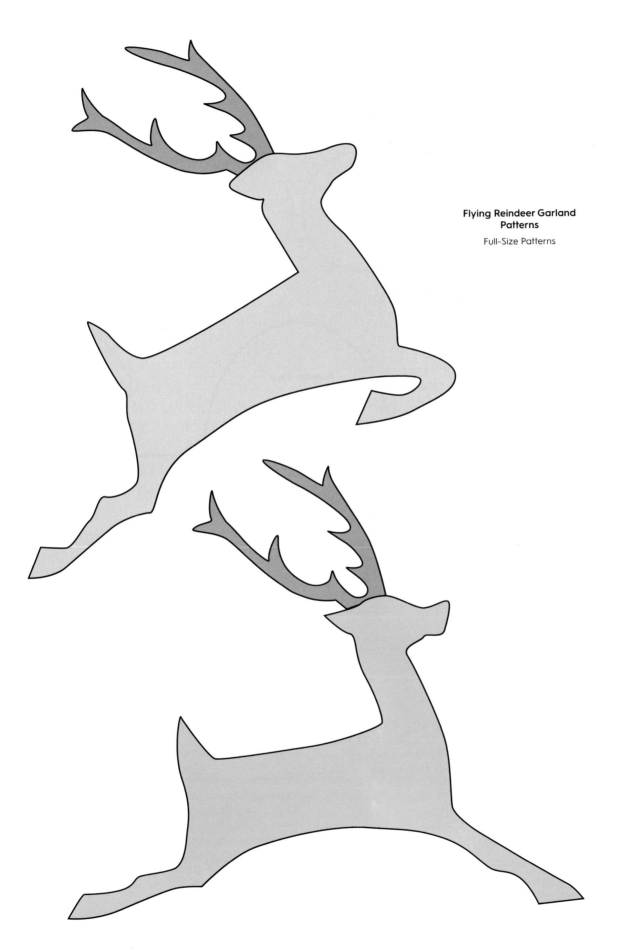

**Flying Reindeer Garland
Patterns**

Full-Size Patterns

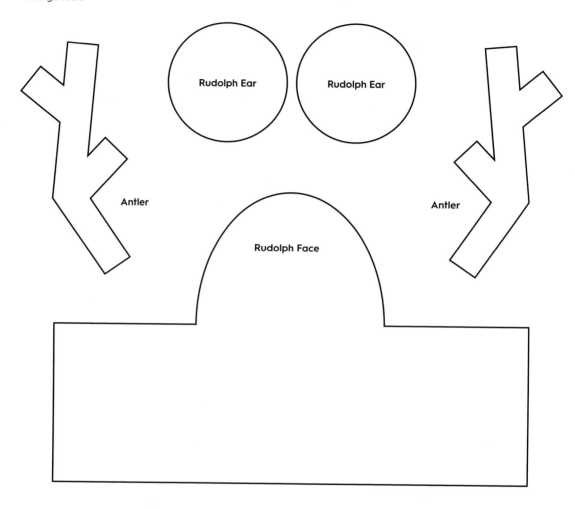

Felt Rudolph Pillow Patterns

Enlarge 300%

Rudolph Ear

Rudolph Ear

Antler

Antler

Rudolph Face

FELT RUDOLPH PILLOW

WHAT YOU NEED

Tracing paper • Pencil • Scissors • Nonwoven felt such as National Nonwovens (light gray for pillow front, pillow back 1, and pillow back 2; dark brown for reindeer face; light brown for reindeer ears; tan for reindeer antlers) • Large red pom-pom • Brown thread or thread to match fabrics • Sewing machine • Two black buttons • 14-inch pillow form • Hot-glue gun and glue sticks

WHAT YOU DO

1. Enlarge template pieces, above, and cut out. Cut pieces according to templates. To create pillow front, pillow back 1, and pillow back 2, cut the following pieces: For pillow front cut one 15×15-inch piece of gray fabric. For pillow back cut two 15×10-inch pieces.

2. Position reindeer face on top of pillow front by lining up the bottoms of the pieces and pin in place. Fold reindeer ears in half. Pin in place, tucking them under the reindeer face. Position reindeer antlers and pin in place, tucking them under the reindeer face.

3. Stitch down the center of the reindeer antlers. When both reindeer antlers have been stitched to pillow front, stitch around the perimeter of reindeer face to secure reindeer face and reindeer ears to pillow front using a ½-inch seam.

4. With right sides together, align the top of pillow back 1 with the top of pillow front. Align the bottom of pillow back 2 with the bottom of pillow front. Stitch around the entire pillow, allowing a ½-inch seam allowance.

5. Turn right side out. Attach pom-pom and buttons with a hot-glue gun. Insert pillow form.

WOODLAND FRIENDS

Scrap pieces of birch and other favorite woods combine to make some reindeer for Santa's sleigh.

WHAT YOU NEED

Small pieces of birch or other soft wood • Small sticks of desired wood • Small sticks that resemble branches for antlers • Small handsaw • Drill with drill bits to match size of wood • Pen knife (optional) • Hot-glue gun and glue sticks • Red or brown small round sticker

WHAT YOU DO

1. Plan the design of the reindeer. Cut the pieces of wood for the body and the head. Cut the leg and neck pieces. Trim the antler pieces.

2. Drill holes in the body and head pieces to match the size of the legs, neck, and antlers. Use a pen knife if necessary to whittle the ends to fit.

3. Put the ends into the holes, using a dot of hot glue to hold if needed.

4. Add a nose using a small round sticker.

CROSS-STITCH REINDEER PENDANT

Tiny stitches line up to make a sweet reindeer motif to wear or share.

WHAT YOU NEED

Embroidery thread in brown and red • Predrilled wooden circle pendant (see Sources, page 160) • Embroidery needle • Cording such as bakers twine

WHAT YOU DO

1. Using three strands of embroidery thread, use the template pattern, right, to work the design on the purchased circle pendant. Tie off threads on back of pendant.

2. Attach to a cord for hanging.

Cross-Stitch Reindeer Pendant Template

FELT REINDEER POUCHES

Deer-motif felt pouches make darling party favors or the perfect gift card or money holder.

WHAT YOU NEED

Tracing paper • Pencil • Scissors • Wool felt such as National Nonwovens in desired colors • Needles: embroidery and sewing • Thread to match fabrics • Embroidery floss in desired colors • ¾-inch-diameter wooden button • Felt glue such as Beacon's Felt Glue

WHAT YOU DO

1. Enlarge pouch patterns, opposite, onto white paper; cut out. Trace pattern and cut one pouch from desired colors of felt. With right sides together and using a ³⁄₁₆-inch seam allowance, sew flap to pouch along sewing line shown on pattern. Fold flap over; press.

2. Fold pouch on fold line; press. Cut buttonhole slit on flap where indicated on pattern. Using red embroidery floss, sew button in place and blanket-stitch together sides of pouch. Glue reindeer head to back of pouch; let dry.

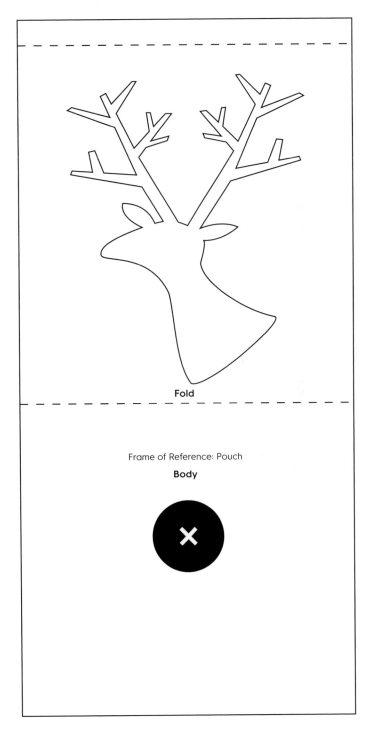

Fold

Frame of Reference: Pouch

Body

*Use your favorite colors
of nonwoven felt to make
these festive and handy little
pouches that can be used in
so many ways.*

REINDEER GREETING

A simple reindeer makes the perfect motif for a Christmas greeting card.

WHAT YOU NEED

Tracing paper • Pencil • Scissors • Blank card and envelope • Scrap of brown cardstock • Scrap of contrasting piece of cardstock • Crafts glue • Ribbon with a message • Tiny jingle bell • Needle • Bakers twine • Red and black beads (optional)

WHAT YOU DO

1. Trace the template, right, and cut out. Copy onto brown cardstock and cut out.
2. Cut a piece of contrasting paper in a shape to resemble land. Glue to the blank card at the bottom. Glue the reindeer on top.
3. Cut the ribbon to fit along the bottom of the card. Glue ribbon in place.
4. Use the needle to punch a hole on both sides of the reindeer neck. Thread the bell onto the bakers twine and pull the twine through the holes, tying at the back.
5. Glue a nose and eye on the reindeer if desired.

Reindeer Greeting Pattern

Full-Size Pattern

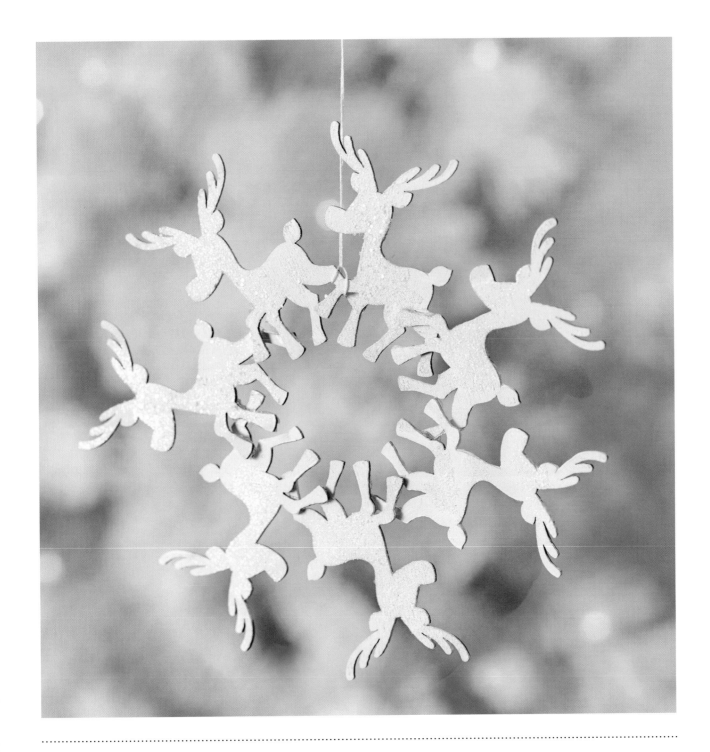

REINDEER GAMES MINI WREATH
Little reindeer shapes circle around to form a simple wreath to hang in a window or doorway.

WHAT YOU NEED
Small purchased wood reindeer shapes (available at crafts stores) • White spray paint • Hot-glue gun and glue sticks • Fine white glitter • White cord

WHAT YOU DO
1. Plan the design of the wreath by laying out the wood deer pieces. Lay them on a covered surface and spray with white paint. Let dry.
2. Use hot glue to glue the pieces together, slightly overlapping the pieces.
3. Paint the pieces again and dust with glitter while wet. Let dry.
4. Add a cord at the top for hanging.

Door Pleasers

Greet your guests with a simple or an elegant wreath to brighten your holiday door decor.

BOTTLEBRUSH-TREE STAR
Bottlebrush trees reposition themselves to create a star for your front door.

WHAT YOU NEED
Bottlebrush trees in desired colors and sizes • Plastic foam half circle such as Styrofoam to fit size of trees • Hot-glue gun and glue sticks • Small round ornaments to coordinate with tree • Ribbon

WHAT YOU DO
1. Plan the design of the star by laying the trees around the plastic foam half circle. **Note:** We used seven trees for a 3-inch circle and six trees for a 2-inch circle.
2. Push the trees into the side of the plastic foam circle and use a dot of hot glue to hold if necessary. Continue until the star shape is complete.
3. Hot-glue the small ornaments to the plastic foam circle in the center of the trees.
4. Attach a ribbon at the top for hanging.

JINGLE, JINGLE DOORKNOB PLEASER

Make a little Christmas music every time you open the door with this easy-to-make door decoration.

WHAT YOU NEED

Fresh greenery • Jingle bells in desired colors • Wire • Narrow ribbon • Wide burlap ribbon

WHAT YOU DO

1. Lay the greenery on a flat surface and wire together at the top to create a greenery swag.

2. Thread the bells on wire and wire them to the swag.

3. Tie the narrow ribbon at the top and curl the ends. Tie burlap ribbon in a large bow above the narrow ribbon.

4. Add wire or ribbon at the top for hanging.

CANDY CANE DOOR WELCOME

Greet guests with a little sugar, all tied up with striped ribbon bows.

WHAT YOU NEED

Candy canes • Wire • Red-and-white striped ribbon • Fresh greenery • Red berries

WHAT YOU DO

1. Fan out the candy canes and wire together in the middle.

2. Tie a bow around the candy canes, tucking in the greenery and the berries.

3. Loop another piece of ribbon around the candy canes for hanging, tying a bow at the top.

BERRY-POMEGRANATE WREATH

A simple grapevine wreath is adorned with fresh pomegranates to make a stunning door pleaser.

WHAT YOU NEED

12-inch grapevine wreath • Bag of green sheet moss • Hot-glue gun and glue sticks • Wooden skewer • 5 fresh pomegranates • Florists wire • 10 to 12 pinecones • Real or faux winterberry in various sizes, (about thirty 8-inch branches)

WHAT YOU DO

1. Cover the wreath with sheet moss and glue in place. Use the wooden skewer to place a hole through the base of each pomegranate. Thread florists wire through each piece of fruit and wire to the front of the wreath, spacing the fruit evenly around the circle.

2. Glue two pinecones between each pomegranate. Insert berry branches into the wreath, varying the sizes and placement. Glue to secure in place.

GREEN LEAF WREATH

*Snippets of felt in all shades of green combine to make a
simple-but-sweet door decoration.*

WHAT YOU NEED

Tracing paper • Pencil• Scissors • Wire wreath form • Felted
balls (see Sources, page 160) • Nonwoven felt in shades of
green • Florists wire • Hot-glue gun and glue sticks • Silver
beads

WHAT YOU DO

1. Referring to the template patterns, right, cut leaves out of
felt. Set aside. Cut the florists wire to about 8 inches. To create
strings of leaves, apply a dab of hot glue to the bottom tip or
outward tip (depending on petal) of the petal where indicated
on the template. Attach it to the top of the florists wire,
pressing the sides around to meet each other. Add additional
leaves, staggering them slightly on the wire.

2. Wrap florists wire with the leaves on it, around the wire
wreath form. Embellish the wreath with felted balls and silver
beads, applying with hot glue. Add small dots of green felt to
the felt balls if desired.

Green Leaf Wreath Patterns

Full-Size Patterns

● = Glue

TRADITIONAL SWAGGER

Studded with red berries and topped with a big red bow, this swag is sure to become a much-loved classic. For fullness, a long-needle teardrop-shape base anchors the arrangement.

WHAT YOU NEED

Long-needle teardrop-shape swag with pinecones • 2 large faux mixed-pine sprays • Florists wire • Pinecones (optional, depending on how many pinecones your swag has) • 1⅔ yards of 2-inch-wide wire-edged red ribbon • Faux red berries on stems • Hot-glue gun and glue sticks

WHAT YOU DO

1. Lay the swag on your work surface. Center the mixed-pine sprays vertically on the swag, placing one spray pointing toward the top and one toward the bottom (with stems meeting toward the middle). Wire the sprays to the swag. Use florists wire to attach additional pinecones as you like to the middle of the swag, centering them on the swag vertically and slightly below center.

2. Use florists wire to attach a bow made from the red ribbon, placing it toward the top of the swag just above the pinecones. To make the bow, cut a 40-inch length of ribbon. Leaving a 10-inch tail, make a 5-inch loop, holding the ribbon between your thumb and index finger. Continue holding the ribbon and make a second loop the same size in the opposite direction. Continue until you have six loops. Wrap wire around the bow center, not trimming the wire ends. For the remaining bow tails, wire the remaining piece of ribbon to the center. Trim the wire and ribbon ends.

3. Hot-glue red berries to the swag, fanning out on the swag center.

SIDESWEPT SOPHISTICATION WREATH

WHAT YOU NEED

14-inch grapevine wreath • 3 faux mixed-pine spray • Hot-glue gun and glue sticks • 1⅔ yards of 2½-inches-wide wire-edge burlap ribbon • Florists wire • Faux red berries • Faux peppermint greenery • Faux willow branches

WHAT YOU DO

1. Hot-glue the mixed-pine sprays to the left side of the wreath. Wire a bow made from the burlap ribbon to the left side of the wreath. Position the bow slightly above center. To make the bow, cut a 40-inch length of ribbon. Leaving a 14-inch tail, make a 4-inch loop, holding the ribbon between your thumb and index finger. Continue holding the ribbon and make 5-inch loops in both directions. Continue holding the ribbon and make 6-inch loops in both directions. Wrap wire around the bow center, not trimming the wire ends. For the remaining bow tails, wire the remaining piece of ribbon to the center. Trim the wire and ribbon ends.

2. Hot-glue or wire the red berries to the left side of the wreath, working upward, sideways, and downward from the bow.

3. Hot-glue peppermint greenery to the left side of the wreath, working upward, downward, and sideways for the bow. Let the vines trail down and off the wreath.

4. Hot-glue willow branches to the left side of the wreath, positioning them so they flow naturally from the top and bottom of the wreath.

FELT BLOOMS WREATH

Layers of felt become lovely little blooms that line up to make a soft and welcoming wreath for your holiday door.

WHAT YOU NEED

Tracing paper • Pencil • Scissors • Flat wreath form • Nonwoven felt such as National Nonwovens in desired colors • Hot-glue gun and glue sticks • Small beads in desired colors

WHAT YOU DO

1. Trace petal templates and cut out. Cut all shapes from desired colors of felt.

2. To make a single flower, attach the center of petals (of the same size) around a circle using hot glue.

3. Arrange flowers in desired pattern around the wreath form using hot glue. Glue beads in groupings to the centers of the flowers where desired.

Felt Blooms Wreath Patterns

Full-Size Patterns

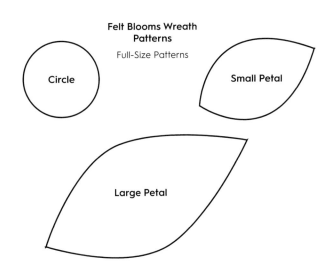

Circle

Small Petal

Large Petal

PRETTY PASTEL PINECONE WREATH

Tiny pinecones combine with wooden roses and mini ball ornaments to make a retro color wreath for the holidays.

WHAT YOU NEED

Purchased pinecone wreath or make your own • Wood roses (instructions, right) • Crafts paint in pink and teal • Paintbrush • Small ball ornaments in soft green, pink, and teal • Spray paint in white and gold • Hot-glue gun and glue sticks • Wide hot-pink ribbon • Fresh greenery • Wire • Scissors

WHAT YOU DO

1. Lay the wreath on a flat surface to plan the design. Decide how many wood roses will be needed. To make the wood roses, use a wood plane or draw knife to shave wood curls from a soft wood such as poplar. **Note:** We used a 1-inch-thick piece of poplar, planing along the short edge. Paint the wood curls with pink or teal crafts paint and let dry.

2. Remove the pinecones where the rose curls and ornaments are to go.

3. Spray-paint the wreath white leaving some areas natural. Let dry. Spray some fresh greens white. Let dry.

4. Hot-glue the wood roses and little ornaments where the pinecones were removed. Hot-glue the greenery at the top of the wreath.

5. Add wire or ribbon at the top for hanging. Make a bow and wire to the top of the wreath.

STITCH DIAGRAMS

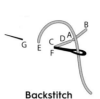

Backstitch

Straight Stitch

Chain Stitch

Whipstitch

French Knot

Buttonhole Stitch

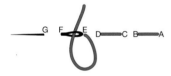

Running Stitch

Fern Stitch

Star Stitch

Stem Stitch

KNITTING ABBREVIATIONS

BEG begin (ning)
DEC decrease
INC increase
K knit
LP loop
M1 make one or to increase one
P purl
SSK slip, slip knit
TOG together

SOURCES

Crafts Paint
deltacreative.com
plaidonline.com

Cardstock/Scrapbooking Supplies
hobbylobby.com
michaels.com

Paper Tape/Ribbon
cutetape.com

Flower Punch
EKSuccess
Amazon.com

Spray Paint:
walmart.com
menards.com

Wood Slices
michaels.com

Felt
National Nonwovens
nationalnonwovens.com

Glue
Aleene's Tacky Glue
aleenes.com

Beads
michaels.com
joann.com

Papers and Stickers
Memory Bound Scrapbook
 Store, Ankeny, Iowa
 memoryboundscrapbook
 store.com
michaels.com
hobbylobby.com

Bakers Twine
hobbylobby.com

Felt Balls
craftywoolfelt.com

Reindeer Pendant
Amazon.com /Dimensions

Ribbon
offray.com

CROCHET ABBREVIATIONS

BEG begin (ning)
CH chain
DC double crochet
HDC half double crochet
INC increase
SC single crochet
SL ST slip stitch
ST(S) stitch(es)

CRAFT DESIGNERS

Meredith Armand • Judy Bailey • Lindsey Berger • Jan Carlson • Carol Field Dahlstrom • Roger H. Dahlstrom • Jackie Dickey • Linda Goodin • Jodi Harris • Kim Hutchison • Pam Koelling • Heather Kowalski • Katie Leporte • Janet Pittman • Amy Sinibaldi • Jan Temeyer